C000283365

LYNNE'S LAWS OF LEADERSHIP

20 BIG LESSONS FOR LEADING A SMALL LAW FIRM

Lynne Burdon

First published in Great Britain by Practical Inspiration Publishing, 2018

© Lynne Burdon, 2018

The moral rights of the author have been asserted

ISBN 978-1-78860-029-3

All rights reserved. This book, or any portion thereof, may not be reproduced without the express written permission of the author.

Every effort has been made to trace copyright holders and to obtain their permission for the use of copyright material. The publisher apologizes for any errors or omissions and would be grateful if notified of any corrections that should be incorporated in future reprints or editions of this book.

Table of Contents

PRAISE FOR LYNNE'S RULES

This book is a treasure-trove of insight and wisdom. Every page is teeming with the benefits of 30 years of hard work - the lived experience of 'been there, done that' through many excitements and challenges. The role of managing partner in a law firm can be a lonely one at times. Few others will fully appreciate the nature or the pressure of the decisions and actions that have to be taken, sometimes with imperfect information and almost always against the clock. This book will be like having a coach and mentor by your side as a constant guide and companion.

For most rational, left-brained lawyers, the affirmation of the need for a clear purpose, vision and strategy will be welcome news. So, too, the advice to focus individuals and the firm on what they are truly good at. And the drive for the proper pay-off and returns for personal and collective efforts will undoubtedly resonate. But there is something more important here, too. You cannot finish Lynne's Laws without understanding the power of passion and a 'good fit': those positive, driving, motivating forces so often overlooked or under-valued in professional services businesses, but without which the working environment can be such a soulless, enervating place. The so-called 'soft skills' (that in fact underpin everything in organisations populated by infinitely varied, idiosyncratic, and temperamental human beings - however talented they might otherwise be) are shown here time and time again to have a purpose and a value that is disproportionate to their perceived worth.

The style throughout these pages is direct, personal and compelling. It is also generous in sharing the learning and reflections from three decades of building and sustaining organisational coherence and success through a period of profound change in legal practice.

You cannot fail to be impressed by it, to learn from it and even, on occasion, to be moved by it.

Professor Stephen Mayson, author of Making Sense of Law Firms and Law Firm Strategy: Competitive Advantage and Valuation

This is a fantastic resource for anyone involved in law firm management, whether just starting out on that lonely road, or an old timer like me. Lynne has obviously thought deeply and read widely on the subject over the years. She brilliantly distils the essence of what she has learned from this and from her practical experience to produce a very readable book, peppered with entertaining and informative anecdotes which really bring to life the lessons she has learned and is now passing on.

Lynne rightly says that in business planning you should pay attention more to your own strengths and the opportunities in the market than to your competitors, but if I did create a list of our top competitors, then it is a tribute to Lynne's leadership that both of her firms would certainly be on it.

David Marshall, Managing Partner, Anthony Gold Solicitors

Using her two law firms as a 30-year case study, Lynne uncovers what it takes to create a truly great business – the passion, the rigour, the courage and self-belief. Using real examples she shares her wisdom and experience, her failures and successes, to tell the story of how her firm grew – and the invaluable lessons it taught her.

Lynne explores with striking clarity what she has learned about how all this works (or sometimes doesn't!), and why it is so important.

She has created an invaluable handbook for others – a practical guide for how to build a great law firm, an ethical workplace, and a life that is meaningful and fun. And the things you need to do each and every day to keep it that way.

This book is a rich treasure of business theory brought to life with flesh-and-blood examples. If you haven't got time for an MBA, you should certainly read this book.

Des O'Connell, Sherwood PSF Consulting
(ex-managing partner of a City law firm)

This is a remarkable achievement. It combines a hugely readable personal story of the founder of a successful law firm with a detailed clear and very practical 'how to do it manual' full of transferable ideas for anyone who wants to learn about leadership.

Lynne's passion and principles shine through and are allied with a healthy dose of pragmatism as well as lacking the hubris that sometimes mars other such monographs.

The contents list reads like one from any business school 'syllabus' on how to set up and sustain a successful professional services firm - including in a period of constant change. All the 'laws' are evidence based - ie supported by both research and experience; moreover unlike some 'this is how I did it' texts, Lynne explains in some detail how she went about putting them into practice (using stories of successes and mistakes in equal measure) and thereby makes them transferable beyond her own context. It seems to me that her advice is relevant to any business that depends for success on delivering the highest level of client service and creating a group of highly engaged and talented group of people who want to do just that. At the end of each chapter she asks a 'few great questions' as a good starting point for reflection and action (and a useful summary of the Law in question).

This is a fascinating read – full of stories and wise advice shared with serious intent and a touch of humour throughout.

Sally Woodward, Solicitor, Business and Leadership Coach
Founding Principal Sherwood PSF Consulting

If anyone was going to write a book about being a managing partner, Lynne is the ideal candidate. She's a powerhouse.

Her unbridled energy, infectious enthusiasm and likeable personality means that she relates to clients, staff and suppliers alike in the most positive way. And reading it from the perspective of an accountant who has been in practice (and running one) for many years, what she has to say in her book doesn't just apply to law firms. The easily digestible information that Lynne has shared here is a must read for any managing partner of a professional services company or firm, anyone aspiring to lead such an organisation and anyone working in the professions. In fact, it's just an enlightening read for any one of us working in commerce today.

Jeff Gitter, Senior Partner, Lubbock Fine Chartered Accountant

All too often, books on leadership and success are written by managers, people who, by definition, mostly tend to be great at following the directives, strategies and systems set by the visionaries and leaders they work for. That's not to say that management isn't an important or even vital skill set within the operating of any successful operation or business, but it sometimes seems to me that there are already plenty of books out there aimed at efficiency, scale and other aspects of the management skillset, yet far too few that get into the genuine nitty-gritty of what goes on in the mind of someone focused on the big-picture, helicopter-view of a business that marks out the true leader and visionary.

In the pages of this book, Lynne lifts back the curtain on the exact philosophies, principles and practices she employed over the years – the good, the bad and the ugly – and shares them in a practical, use-the-next-day manner that will get the reader thinking differently about how they can create an environment and culture where success can thrive naturally and without all of the control, limitation and restriction so common in organisations these days.

If you've been looking for a way to create more impact, more influence and more inspiration both within your business and the niche it serves, you'll really enjoy some of the truth-bombs Lynne's Laws will be dropping on you.

Dax Moy, Founder, MindMAP Mastery Coaching Institute
National Academy of Best-Selling Authors 'Quilly' Recipient
***Author of* The MAGIC Hundred**

Dedicated to Louise and Jonathan

It is with total confidence that I say you will both be better managing partners than me. I am proud of that.

Thank you to the people who have shaped me

I wouldn't have been the managing partner I was without my co-founder Roger Bolt. Roger, thank you for the always available shoulder to cry on and for your unending confidence that I could do it no matter how tough the times were.

I have to thank my amazing children Joe and Jenny who sacrificed more than anyone while their mum was busy being a managing partner.

There are three people who have changed how I see the world: David Shepherd, who taught me all my NLP – I use it everywhere mostly unconsciously which of course is just how he would like it; Stephen Mayson, who opened my eyes to a wealth of academic thought and research on business leadership on his amazing MBA course; and the incredible Dax Moy, my coach now for many years – his wisdom is everywhere in this book.

From my own firms I need to thank: all our clients who trusted us with their life problems, our only wish was to make your lives better and in the very few cases we failed I am truly sorry; all my current partners who took the risk and joined us in this incredible journey; and most importantly all the wonderful people who work for us now and who have done so in the past – it is for you and from you that I have learnt everything I write.

Finally I must also thank my publisher Alison Jones and the team at Practical Inspiration Publishing, Julia Slone–Murphy of NeuroEdit Ltd, who helped me shape my thoughts into a book, and Simon Thompson of Aubrey Design for his illustrations.

Introduction

Many times over the past 30 years I have been asked what it is like to be the managing partner – I don't think I have ever answered that question publicly with total honesty till now. Managing a small law firm can be scary, lonely, stressful, overwhelming and confusing. It is also the most magical, satisfying, wonderful and rewarding job I could ever have dreamed of.

I can only talk about small firms because that is where my experience is. When I say 'small' I mean with total staff of up to 150 people. So not very small! There are several reasons why 150 is the magic number – read on to find out!

I remember so clearly that passion we had when we started Bolt Burdon back in 1986. It is fortunate that we didn't know what we didn't know – because if we had I am not sure we would have had the courage to go ahead. But we did understand the most important things even then – that for clients we must have the highest standards of ethics and give practical legal advice coupled with exceptional standards of service. And that we also wanted to create a great place to work, where everyone shared our beliefs and where we could have fun together. A place that would use the best technology and where innovation was happening all the time for the benefit of our clients and our people.

Now as I pass on the baton to others I am able to reflect and talk honestly about my journey – the joys I have experienced and the lessons I have learnt. I want to make sure that the lessons I have learnt are remembered for the benefit of the firms I love.

This is a very personal book about my experiences in my own firms. It is written to help those who follow me and in the hope that other readers find things to translate to their own organisations.

Over the last 30 years I have learnt a lot. I have taken my leadership career seriously with traditional learning, including an MBA, and by less traditional routes including the study of NLP (neuro-linguistic programming) and more recently the study of neuroscience to learn more about how our amazing human brains work.

However, I believe the best learning is done by tackling real-life challenging projects, and reflecting on your results. Running a law firm is certainly a challenging project and in this book I hope to share my experiences, offer advice on how I now see the world and give guidance on how others can tackle the same issues.

In this book I offer the top 20 lessons I have learnt for effective leadership during my 30 years as managing partner. I integrate my stories and experience that have, after reflection, led me to my Rules that I believe have universal application.

I have arranged the Rules in a logical order: Rules 1 to 6 deal with big picture issues; Rules 7 to 11 deal with employing staff; Rules 12 and 13 with partnership matters and then Rules 14 to 19 with some everyday guidance; Rule 20 may be the most important of all – my rule for living your best life!

The real value in this book for you will be reflecting on the 'great questions' at the end of each Rule and working out your own rules for your team or organisation.

Although my book is about running a law firm the principles apply equally to running any business or team where client service and attracting and retaining the best people are the critical factors.

This book puts an end to my career as a managing partner – recording my legacy, if you like.

Its publication frees me up to focus on my new career as a coach and mentor to law firm leaders and to offer training to help make law firms happier places to work.

Visit my website at **www.lynneburdon.com** to learn more about how you can work with me.

Reading note

When I say 'us' I mean one or both of my law firms, Bolt Burdon (**www.boltburdon.co.uk**) or Bolt Burdon Kemp (**www.boltburdonkemp.co.uk**). Most things in this book apply equally to both but sometimes I am drawing from the experience of just one and sometimes just the other. I tend to say 'firm' rather than 'firms' because that will make more sense to the reader.

I have changed some of the anecdotes sufficiently to protect the guilty, changing status, gender, times, etc.

The stories about me are completely true!

Rule 1:
Never forget why you bother

Running a law firm is hard work. It's a big job, and it often means working long hours. It takes great strength and courage. There are bound to be sacrifices and hard choices to make: a weekend at home with the family, or a weekend in the office making sure the cash flow forecast is right before it goes to the bank on Monday? There will be many difficult decisions to take: decisions that affect the lives of others; decisions to borrow huge sums of money, with your family home on the line; decisions to terminate someone's employment or even close down a whole team, putting the livelihood of others at risk. There will be times when it feels incredibly lonely, and when you'll wish you had a boss to talk to, someone who'd tell you what to do; but the buck stops with you!

It is important to be honest with yourself. Being a business leader is a choice – and you are free to make it. It will only be worth it if you know why you're bothering. This is the heart of the matter. There always has to be a reason why you make that choice – why you get up off your backside, roll up your sleeves and get on with the job. There has to be a strong internal drive; something that makes you want to make the choice. A feeling you're seeking; something that makes all the effort worthwhile.

When you bother – and get it right – the rewards are enormous. There is no better feeling than the joy of a huge success for a client, or a new team becoming profitable, or when, as your staff head home after a really great office party, you hear them say 'This is a brilliant place to work!'

If you're clear why the business exists, and you passionately believe in that, you will want to bother.

1.1. Why we bothered

Roger Bolt and I opened the doors to Bolt Burdon on 1 May 1986.

We'd been partners together in our old firm for several years, having both qualified there and progressed quickly to partnership. It was a good firm in many ways. There were some excellent lawyers, and we had many interesting legal discussions. The training was excellent, and articled clerks and junior solicitors were given lots of responsibility. Most clients were happy, although work was delivered mostly at the convenience of the lawyer, rather than the client, which was pretty much expected in those days.

But in so many other ways, it was at odds with our idea of a great place to work. There were a lot of rules, many unwritten. Everyone was on first-name terms, except the partners, who insisted on being called Mister. It was expected that articled clerks would work long hours and I never felt comfortable leaving the office before the partner I was working for went home. Lunch was strictly one hour, during which the partners went home and the phones were switched off. A group of us always went out to lunch together; it was a welcome break in the middle of a long day, and we often took more than the allocated hour. Nothing was ever said; instead, we'd arrive back to the building to find the lights switched off in our offices – a clear demonstration of disapproval. I was working long days, regular 12-hour stretches, and I routinely worked Saturdays. It was very annoying and very demotivating.

Roger and I had lots of ideas for improvement. We were always suggesting changes. We had to fight hard for the first word processer to be bought. We thought that solicitors should specialise, as it was difficult to keep up to date with all areas of law. We wanted to open a second office, and even found a site, but the other partners weren't interested. We wanted more of a social life around work but even the budget for the Christmas lunch was a battle every year. We often talked together about how we'd like to change the firm. Unlike our other partners, we were hungry and we wanted more – more challenge, more fun and more money!

As we spent time together, working long hours and sharing our hopes and dreams for the future we sometimes discussed starting a firm of our own but it just didn't seem possible. We would have to start completely from scratch – without any of our clients because of covenants in our partnership deed. It was a partnership dispute that eventually gave us our chance. To resolve the dispute Roger and I offered to leave on terms that would allow us to take all our current work and clients with us.

We'd been given the chance of a lifetime. This was our opportunity to create the firm of our dreams. Could we create something really different? The idea of building our own firm was so exciting to us. It would be a place where clients were important and staff were trusted and valued, and where there was a feeling that we could all thrive and grow together. We were thrilled and terrified.

As it happened, we were unexpectedly given an alternative. During the dispute, we'd taken legal advice from a very well-known partnership lawyer. He was so impressed with our billing figures that he offered us both partnerships in his firm! We knew this would be the safe option, the prestigious option, and possibly the more financially rewarding option, and we considered his offer carefully... for about five minutes. There really was no doubt in our minds. We were so excited about doing our own thing that it was easy to turn down this very attractive offer. And so we began to realise our dream.

We were young and naïve – I was just 30 at the time. We knew we had a lot to learn about running a business, and we were determined to learn and succeed.

Why did we want this so much? Why did we bother? No one asked us why at the time, but if they had, I think we would have said:

> *'We want to improve the lives of our clients. We want to give the very best practical legal advice with the highest ethical standards (always putting the clients' best interests first) coupled with amazing levels of client service, working to suit our clients' schedules rather than our own.'*

and

> *'We want to create a great place to work – a place where everyone can flourish. We want only to work with people who share our passion and our values. People who strive to be great lawyers and provide excellent service. People who are ready to go the extra mile for our clients, working weekends if needed. People who are constantly innovating and learning and looking for better ways of*

> *doing things. We want to be a team; a family – ev*
> *pulling together. We want to have fun with our colle*
> *both in and out of the office.'*

From all the clients we invited to follow us from our old firm, only one said no (our new office was too far for her to travel). We were delighted – this was overwhelming evidence that we must be doing something right!

1.2. The 'core ideology'

Over 30 years later, nothing has changed – what I wanted then is still exactly what I want for our business now.

A key moment for me was in 1998 when I came across *Built to Last* by Jim Collins and Jerry I Porras[1] in my local bookshop. I took it home and read it from cover to cover, unable to put it down. Its central concept is that truly visionary companies have a 'core ideology' – a combination of 'core purpose' and 'core values' that sit at the heart of the company and which will never change. This core ideology is the reason why the business exists. Reading this felt like someone completely understood us. The feeling that Roger and I had when thinking about our business was so strong – we were so passionate about it – that we would do absolutely anything to achieve this dream. And we would rather close the firm down than let go of this 'core ideology'.

Later Simon Sinek published *Start with Why.*[2] In it, he suggests a similar thing – that every business has a reason why it exists and that the business is one of the things that its founders have done to live their own life purpose. I do believe we all have a life purpose – the reason we exist – the way in which we want to make our lives meaningful and make our difference in this world. That's what Roger and I were doing. We were creating a vehicle for our respective life purposes. To make it a success, all we needed to do was attract others to come and work with us who could live their own life purpose in the environment of our 'core ideology'.

More recently, I've learnt why this reason for existing is so important, and why it evokes so much feeling in me. There's an ancient part of our brain (our 'mammalian' brain) that's concerned with bonding and caring for our young and other members of our tribe. This is where feelings and emotions live. We're wired to want to be part of a tribe. It's why we feel good when we're with others who think the same as we do, and why we care so much about what other people think; it's our mammalian brain trying to prevent us from getting thrown out of the gang.

Our brain is constantly scanning the environment, looking for danger and seeking safety. We all search for other people like us; and when we find them, neurochemicals are released that cause us to feel warmth and trust. This is the reason that when we recognise a business with a 'why' that fits with our own life purpose, it feels good. We feel like we're in the right tribe. Everyone wants this; it gives us a sense of belonging and makes us feel safe.

This is why it's critical that you, as a business leader, are really clear about why your business exists. If you're not, you'll face all sorts of problems in leading your business. You won't be able to create that feeling of belonging to a tribe, because the tribe has no core reason to exist. You'll have no clear sense of direction; you won't know what to do next. You'll struggle to communicate to your staff what's important to your business, and you'll watch them leave as they discover for themselves that they're in the wrong tribe. As a result of all these things, the performance of your business will begin to suffer.

But when the 'why' of the business is clear, that 'core ideology' will be at the heart of every business decision. Each potential recruit will have the information to decide for themselves whether or not this is a business aligned with their own personal 'why', a place where they'll be able to follow their own passion. People motivated by the business 'why' will be attracted to it, ar who are not will look elsewhere. Those who are motiv your 'core ideology' will feel like they're at home, in the right tribe. Every member of the team will have a grand and aspirational common purpose to rally around – one that is truly motivating. Every person working in the organisation will be living their own life purpose while being totally committed to the business purpose too. What a powerful business that makes.

For each of us, there will be many organisations in which our personal 'why' can be satisfied, because it's in alignment with the business purpose. What is important is that the business in which we are working is one of them! For a founder, that is bound to be so. For everyone else, if you're passionate about what you do, then you can be certain you're living your business life in alignment with your own life purpose as it stands today.

Jim Collins[3] describes a 'relentless, creative drive, a constantly irritating and unreachable itch, about the need to do something valuable and significant for no other reason than that is what it is to be fully human.' That's how it feels to be playing a leading role in a business that's in line with your life purpose.

When your business and life purpose are in alignment, you will make that decision to go to work, no matter what else seems easier, and no matter what stands in your way.

A few great questions

1. Are you clear about your own life purpose? If not, ask yourself: What do you want your life to stand for? What are you passionate about? What makes you really angry? What would you like to change in this world?

2. Are you happy in your job? If so, you are probably aligned with the business's 'why'. If not, what's missing for you?

3. Are you clear what the core ideology of your organisation is? If not, ask the founders, if they're around. If they're long gone, what do you think they would have said? The core ideology will be visible somewhere. If it can't be found, it's time for the top team to settle down to some serious work to restate it.

4. If you're leading a team, do they have some special 'why'? It needs to be in alignment with the organisation 'why' but might include something extra – a reason why this part of the business exists.

Rule 2:

Strategy: The more you focus the better you will do!

Your core ideology – the reason why you exist – will inform some of your highest level strategic choices. We knew from the start that we wanted to be the sort of firm where we all work together for the benefit of the clients. Where the whole is greater than the sum of the parts. Where the focus is on a collaborative approach and long-term success. This then dictates some of our decisions, like sharing profits amongst the partners equally so that we're encouraged to be a collaborative team. It's why we evaluate staff performance on measures that include the level of client delight and contribution to the life of the firm.

However, there are lots of choices left to be made that are not dictated by our reason for existing. Our core ideology says nothing about the sort of work we want to do nor the types of client we want to serve.

2.1. How we got to our choices

When we started Bolt Burdon in 1986, we just picked up our clients from our previous firm and moved them to a new location. We were doing the same sorts of work our previous firm had done. Our strategy was simple – we were lawyers and we would turn our hand to almost any legal problem. It was common for lawyers to give advice in all areas in those days. We specialised a bit – Roger did the litigation and I did non-contentious work. From the outset, we had happy clients and we were making money. At that time, we believed that to be successful we had to provide every possible type of legal service that our clients might want.

If I'd known then what I know now, we would have done it very differently. We had the opportunity for a clean sheet of paper in deciding what sort of work we would do, and we missed that chance. However, over the years since then, we have made many strategic decisions – and nearly all of these have resulted in a narrower focus in the sort of work we do or the types of client we serve.

It was only three years after we started the business that we made the decision to stop doing criminal work. The problem that led to this decision was that one day there were two lots of clients in reception. On one side of the room there were three men in suits, waiting to see me about a company acquisition; on the other was a dishevelled young man waiting to see one of our solicitors because he had been charged with indecent exposure! (Yes, this really happened!) It just didn't feel right. After exploring several options, we realised that, actually, none of us really enjoyed doing the criminal work. It was mostly about facts and evidence, whereas what we were passionate about was using the law. It was then an easy decision to stop doing crime, and we found a good local firm to refer any future clients to. This decision was a relatively easy one as our criminal clients were not normally using us for any other legal services but we were worried about losing an income stream. However, as I think back now I don't recall a single conversation about missing the income stream from criminal legal aid!

In later years we made many other decisions to stop doing certain types of work, including consumer litigation, family work and fast-track personal injury – these always seemed really hard choices at the time, yet looking back, never have we regretted such a decision.

~

The biggest strategic decision I ever made was to divide our firm into two firms.

Roger was passionate about personal injury work. He loved to be David fighting Goliath to recover compensation for clients who had suffered devastating injuries. My passion was helping our commercial and private clients achieve their dreams and life goals. But the fact that we were acting for these two distinct groups of clients caused conflict in two ways. The way to get more personal injury clients was to increase the amount of advertising – which in those days was predominately in the 'Yellow Pages'.[4] Our commercial and private client lawyers did not like this; they thought, quite rightly, that it looked like personal injury was all that we did. The other problem was to do with the working capital requirements of the two sorts of work. Most commercial and private client work was paid for within a few weeks of doing the work. Personal injury cases were often not paid for until they concluded – usually a few years – so this work needed huge amounts of working capital. We found it difficult to attract commercial and private client partners when the capital investment we required from them was so much higher than for firms that didn't do personal injury work.

This was a huge problem, and one we grappled with for several years. Roger and I wanted to hold the firm together – we liked our family all under one roof. We were also very aware of how well the personal injury work had held up during the recession when other areas were struggling. We also had to consider the economies of scale of having one big firm. But the tensions just grew and, in 2003, I decided to split the firm into two firms – now known as Bolt Burdon and Bolt Burdon Kemp, each able to fly in its own direction. We managed to keep some of the economies of scale by setting up a service company so that some support services could still be shared.

That split was one of the best decisions I ever made. Each firm has gone from strength to strength, with its more focused strategy. I'm proud to say that they both still have the same 'core ideology' – how could they not if it was truly at the core?[5]

~

Sometimes external factors have prompted us to re-examine strategy. In 2004, the government-commissioned Clementi Report[6] was published – a review of the regulatory framework for Legal Services, which became known as 'Tesco Law'. It was going to become possible for law firms to be owned by organisations that were not solicitors – possibly household names, like supermarkets, estate agents and insurance companies. This was a significant threat to Bolt Burdon, which, at that time, was a firm acting for a wide range of individuals and businesses. We knew we wouldn't be able to compete with Tesco on price. So we decided that a change of focus was necessary: we would now compete on service. We already offered our clients a great service; we would now hone this even further and act only for businesses and private clients who wanted to pay a premium for exceptional service. This was a big decision but one we felt was essential for the survival of the firm. Our prices and service levels went up. It was sad when clients we had served for some years said they did not want to pay our new prices – but we made sure we identified good firms to refer them to. Once again, we had narrowed our focus.

It was external factors, too, that pushed Bolt Burdon Kemp to cease doing fast-track personal injury work. When we first started personal injury work, public perception was very positive – lawyers helping people in need to recover compensation. The work was funded by legal aid and attracted lawyers who were passionate about their work. In our firm we often jokingly referred to our personal injury lawyers as 'the kaftan brigade' – a slightly unkind jab at their public spiritedness and often left-wing politics. They were passionate about getting compensation for their clients but often not very focused on getting paid themselves! The world changed when legal aid ceased and the 'no win no fee' model arrived. Suddenly everything was different – the commercial world saw the profit in personal injury claims and 'claims farmers' started advertising on TV for claims and selling them on to law firms. Some rogue claims hit the news. Suddenly personal injury lawyers were 'ambulance chasers'. Small claims for minor accidents were now under a fast-track scheme in the courts, with fixed fees. We developed a fast-track team to run these claims efficiently – it was necessary to be very efficient if a profit was to be made. However, this efficiency work didn't fit with our philosophy of being outstanding lawyers with amazing client service. Even worse, the fast-track claims industry had a bad reputation. There were a lot of rogues in this business. We knew backhanders were rife as they were frequently offered to us. We hated being associated with this industry, which the government consistently failed to properly regulate. So we decided to close down our fast-track team. We were worried about this decision – would those who referred clients to us find it odd that we would not deal with minor injuries? On the contrary. As it turned out, the fact we'd specialised further only strengthened our business and reinforced our reputation as serious injury lawyers who handle only the most tragic of cases.

Time and time again, the more focused we were in what we offered, the more successful we became – we had happier clients and we were making more money.

2.2. My four strategic questions

I now think there are four questions law firm leaders need to answer to be clear on strategy:

2.2.1. What is dictated to you by your core ideology?

Whenever there are choices to be made the place to start is with the core ideology – your reason for existing. How does this guide your decision making? What sort of work fits and what is ruled out?

2.2.2. What sort of work will you do, and which clients will you serve?

There are likely to be many sorts of work that fit with your 'why'. You need to make some decisions about what you will do.

Will you just be lawyers, or will you also offer other services, e.g. financial services or estate agency? Will you serve companies or help individuals with their private lives? Maybe you just want to be a property firm, or a litigation firm. Maybe you want to service a particular industry. You will also have to consider what you have – or could develop – the skills to execute. If you want to be a collaborative whole, you will need some sort of link between the areas of work you offer. You will also need to consider how your choices make money – for without a profit there can be no law firm.

In choosing what to do and who to serve I think there are three questions to be considered for a firm (and indeed the same three questions need to be asked by every person who works in the firm):

- What are we passionate about? No one will do their best work if they are not passionate about what they do.
- What are we good at – or what could we become good at? For a small law firm there are going to be some areas that we could never properly service, e.g. corporate work for global corporations.
- What gives us the payoff we are looking for? This will include money but won't only be money. I am absolutely certain that part of the payoff for our personal injury lawyers is the satisfaction of helping people at a time of great tragedy in their lives and I know personally the thrill of helping a client achieve a great business deal or buy the home of their dreams.

The right strategic decisions will be the things that fall within the answers to all three questions – the things we are passionate about, the things we are good at and the things that give us the payoff we are looking for.

In *Good to Great,*[7] Jim Collins describes a similar set of questions in what he calls The Hedgehog Concept. He suggests that the hedgehog knows one big thing: how to roll up into a ball to keep himself safe from the fox. Hedgehogs simplify a complex world into a simple organising idea: a basic principle or concept that unifies and guides everything. I now can't think about top-level strategy without thinking about hedgehogs.

When you have that simple organising idea about who you help or what you do – that is easily explained to clients and staff – I think you have a strong strategy for a law firm.

2.2.3. How will you compete with others who do the same work?

I don't really believe it is helpful to spend too much time considering what your competitors are doing. I have always believed that if you are offering a service that a group of people need and you are clear about exactly what you are offering and you deliver on your promises then you will have a successful business.

Michael Porter[8] suggests there are only three ways to compete: on price (low cost); by differentiation (offering something perceived to be unique); or by focus (serving a particular target market very well). He suggests that effective implementation of any one of these strategies requires total commitment to it.

We have clearly competed on focus. We made a clear decision not to compete on price – we want to act for those who want to pay a premium for service. There is nothing unique about the services we offer – there are many firms that do the same work. We have however given a lot of thought to our target markets and now have real clarity about who it is we are striving to serve.

2.2.4. How must you structure the business to serve the work you do?

Once you know what you are doing you must make decisions about how to structure the firm to best serve the clients.

A firm doing efficiency work, e.g. debt collection or fast-track personal injury, will want to have the best technology and work in highly leveraged teams – maybe one partner managing many unqualified staff. Fees will be low.

At the other end of the spectrum when a client has a very complex and unusual problem where the stakes are very high they will seek the most talented lawyer they can find – and price will not be an important consideration. Such a lawyer will probably work with a small support team around her but most of the work will be done by her personally. This is 'expertise' work.

In between these two extremes of 'efficiency' work and 'expertise' work are most of the issues faced by businesses and individuals. These are important issues but ones that many solicitors will have experience of and be able to do competently. This is 'experience' work. Usually a good structure for this work is small teams of lawyers working together so that the work can be delegated to the most suitable person on the team thus providing excellent service at a reasonable price.

It is difficult to structure a firm for all of these types of work. Further, as David Maister[9] warns, the evolution of practice areas through the stages of the spectrum is becoming very rapid. Work that yesterday was *expertise* work is today *experience* work and will tomorrow be *efficiency* work. Law firms are faced with a choice – follow the work down the spectrum and restructure the practice, or abandon maturing areas of work and move into new practice areas that more closely match the basic approach of the firm.

We have made choices over the years to abandon work which became 'efficiency' work and to focus on 'experience' work.

2.3. So my rule is... The more you focus the better you will do!

What I have learnt over the years is that the more we have focused, the more successful we have been.

- When we made that first decision to narrow focus – to stop doing criminal work – work we did not enjoy – life got better. We were all able to do more of the work we were passionate about.

- When I split the firm in two, this really helped each firm define its focus and allowed each firm to communicate clearly to the world what it did. With that new clarity staff became more motivated and both firms began to build an excellent reputation in their own chosen market. Profits improved.

- At the time of the Clementi Report when we decided to focus even more clearly on acting for clients who only wanted to pay for exceptional service we found we had more happy clients and we became more profitable.

- As we have got clearer and more focused about the clients we want to serve, and we have therefore been able to advertise that, we find we have increasingly distinguished ourselves from our competitors and attracting the right clients to us has become easier.

- As we became increasingly certain that we want to do work only in the 'experience' area we were able to design our structure to support this work. With the right structure in place we have faced fewer client service problems and we have become more profitable.

Today, both our firms now have a really clear focus:

- Bolt Burdon has continued to build on the decision to focus on clients who are willing to pay for the highest level of service delivery and has also now become clearer about the market it does want to serve (rather than what it will not do) – it now focuses on legal services for owner-managed businesses and high-net-worth individuals.

- Bolt Burdon Kemp now works only for clients with the most serious life-changing injuries, with specialist teams for child brain injury, adult brain injury, spinal injury, victims of child abuse, military claims and complex injuries.

A few great questions

1. Are you clear about the strategic decisions that are dictated by your core ideology – the reason why you exist? What is ruled out?

2. Are you doing what you are passionate about, and if not, why not? Do you love your clients, and if not, why are you spending your life with them? How can you focus more on what you love most?

3. Are you doing what you are good at? Are there areas where you could hone your skills even more to better serve your chosen clients?

4. Do you know what 'payoff' you are looking for? Money will be part of it but I believe we all seek something more than this – the things that give our lives meaning.

5. Are you clear about how you compete with those in the market who do the same work? How do you differentiate your firm?

6. Do you do work that is *expertise, experience* or *efficiency* work? Is your work moving down the scale and how are you adapting your structure to that? Or are you choosing to change the work you do so that it fits better with your structure?

Rule 3:
Have a compelling vision to get you out of bed in the mornings

Sometimes, when people look around our lovely offices in Islington, they say to me, 'Lynne, you must be so proud of what you've achieved. Did you ever imagine, when you first started out, that your little law firm would end up as it has?' I can honestly reply that yes, I'm very proud, and yes, I imagined right from the start that it would end up something like this.

I've always known the importance of a good vision – a picture in your head of what the future looks like in your dreams. Even as a young girl, I had my future clearly imagined. I was pony-mad and, back then, my dream was to own a riding school. I can remember every detail of that fantasy: I'm grown up, with my own riding school. But this is no riding school like I have ever seen before. It is beautiful – perfectly arranged around a courtyard. Every pony has its own loose box. The rugs are clean and bright. The tack is polished in a lovely tack room where young girls are chatting happily about the next gymkhana. There are hundreds of rosettes proudly mounted on the wall. There are horses and ponies of all types for all sorts of riders – named after my favourite mounts: Jubbles the black Shetland; Shandy the strawberry roan; Gypsy the steady piebald (or so I thought until she bolted along Redcar beach – the ride of my life!); Major the gray horse for nervous adults; and my favourite, Tigger, a very lively pony prone to all sorts of naughtiness.

Of course, my business of choice changed from a riding school to a law firm, but that same level of detail is what makes a good vision. In my management training sessions, I sometimes tell the story of my childhood vision; when I explain to my staff that they're really just my ponies, this usually raises a giggle!

A clear vision is highly motivating. Almost every author who discusses vision talks about the famous 'I Have a Dream' speech of Martin Luther King. The vivid imagery in that speech can surely leave you in no doubt about the power of a motivating vision. It's essential that you have a clear vision of where you want your business to go.

There is, of course, a scientific reason why a good vision is so motivating. A compelling vision will stimulate the release of dopamine, the neurotransmitter in our brains that makes us strive to achieve something. This will motivate us to take action – and that's important, because a great vision alone achieves nothing; it is only the action we take that makes the difference.

Because of the way our brain works, if a great positive vision is put in your mind, you'll continue to strive for it even when you're not consciously thinking about it. This is why you get the occasional inspiration when walking on the beach, or in the middle of the night. A great vision will motivate everyone who works in the firm. But be under no illusion: the most important person this vision is going to motivate is you – the leader! It's my vision that has got me out of bed every morning for the last 30 years with a spring in my step. 'Oh yes, I want to achieve that. Let's get going!'

Some people are good at seeing a future business in their mind's eye, but for others, getting to a clear vision needs work.

3.1. Before you think about vision

Before embarking on any visioning exercise, it's wise to do two things:

- Remind yourself of the 'core ideology' of the firm – the reason why it exists.

- Think about whether any high-level strategic review is needed. It's difficult to envision a future if you haven't made some decisions at the highest level about the sort of work you're doing and who you're doing it for.

When you're clear about your core ideology and highest-level strategy, you have a strong platform from which to plan your dream future.

3.2. What makes a good vision?

The vision will paint a picture of your business in the future at its very best – why it exists, who it helps and what its values are.

When you get your clear and compelling vision of your future firm, it should evoke emotion – that little lump in your throat as you think about it. It should describe a place you passionately want to work in.

A great vision will be detailed, down to the colour of the carpets, the quality of the canapés and the chat around the kettle – the more detail, the better. And the vision must appeal to all the senses. We all have different preferred modalities for receiving information – preferences for visual, kinaesthetic (touch and feelings), auditory (sound), olfactory (smell), gustatory (taste) or digital information (facts and logic).

So, in describing your vision, be sure to:

- Paint a picture – include shapes and colours. What is the first thing you see as you walk through the door?

- Describe how it feels – the quality of the carpets, the paper the brochure's printed on. How do you think the people are feeling – is there an air of purpose? Do people seem calm, happy, energised, or something else?

- What can you hear? Are people purposefully chatting and laughing? What are they saying? Is there a place of focused silence?

- How does it smell – can you smell that real coffee?

- What is there to taste – is it someone's birthday, and are there donuts in the kitchen? Or maybe a wonderful bowl of fruit?

- And finally, add in some facts and figures to satisfy the digitally minded. How many people do you have, what's the turnover?

The vision is a statement of how you see your business in the future. Avoid comparisons with the present (that comes later).

Express things positively – say what you see, not what you want to avoid.

3.3. Formulating the vision

This is the job of the top team, perhaps with some invited guests. I suggest having fun with this exercise every three years or so, or whenever there's been any change of strategy.

There are many ways of getting to a compelling vision but my favourite is the 'guided visualisation' if you have a team that's 'up for it'! I have found many lawyers are resistant to what they call 'touchy-feely' stuff like this. It's probably because in our day-jobs we use our logical brain more than our creative brain, and we're not so familiar with thinking creatively in this way. However, with the relentless speed of change in the business world, we need to use all the assets we have available.

You need a good facilitator for this. It needs to be done when everyone's in a good mood, and away from the work environment. I think it works really well on the first day of a two-day offsite meeting. As the vision emerges, it's highly motivating. If you're having a partners' offsite meeting, why not invite some guests just for the first part of the 'Vision' day? I suggest getting some input from all generations who work in the firm – select the rising stars.

The way I start is to make sure everyone is in good humour – some 'getting to know you' exercises are good for this, especially if there are people who are not normally in top team meetings. I encourage the cynics to give it a shot and just do the best they can – there is no right way. I suggest they may surprise themselves and enjoy it. I do ask them, though, not to spoil it for others, e.g. by leaving the room half-way through the exercise. If they're not prepared to commit to sitting still and quiet for half an hour, then it's better they leave before you start.

I then ask the group to close their eyes and I take them on a journey. Some slightly hypnotic music helps. The journey is a daydream into the future. On this journey, we happen upon the firm in ten years' time and a miracle has happened – everything has gone as well as it possibly could. By presupposing a miracle, it gives permission to get creative and helps people think big. And because you're talking about a miracle – a phenomenon that's generally considered impossible – people won't really expect to achieve it all, and if they do, they're not thinking big enough!

Going ten years in the future opens the mind to possibilities that might otherwise be dismissed. I think it's far enough in the future to switch off the logical brain – it's too far for calculations like 'If our fee income is £5m and we can add 10% each year, well that's reasonable...'. We don't want step changes. We want to encourage *miracle* thinking.

I ask the team what they see, hear, smell, feel. I offer questions about the building, the people, the clients, the values. For example:

- What type of work is the firm doing? What services are being offered? Who are the clients?

- What sort of people work in the firm? Do you still work there or are you just a visitor? Did you retire or leave? Where do the people work? How much time do they spend in the office? What are people wearing?

- Is there an office building? Where is it? How many people are there today and how many are working elsewhere? What is the turnover? And the profit?

- Who are the business owners? Who made the grade? Is it still a partnership or has the governance structure changed, too?

- Are there any new values? What is the evidence of these?

- How is the firm attracting and keeping the very best people? Generation Y (the Millennials) are probably now firmly in charge and even beginning to think of retirement. What are Generation Z demanding? How is this an amazing place to work for them?

- What big external changes has the firm faced? How did it deal with them? What are the current competitors up to? How have they changed? Who are the competitors now?

- What are people saying? What do your clients say about this firm now? What do the staff say to each other in the pub after work?

- What does the coffee smell like? What else can you smell?

- What happens for fun? How are the firm's sports team doing, and is there still a staff band? What's new?

Finally, I invite people to wonder if this firm in the future has a single big goal or mission. Is there one thing that the firm started to aim for that enabled the miracle to take place?

After some time thinking about the miracle firm ten years in the future, I bring the group back to now. Silence continues and I ask everyone to write down what they saw – in the present tense and in as much detail as possible. I give as much time as necessary for this.

I then ask people to share their dreams, and I begin to capture any common themes. We debate the more outrageous ideas – I really hope there are some! Finally, we discuss time scales – do these ideas need ten years, or can some be implemented much sooner – or need even longer?

You now need to state your vision.

It is 3rd January 2028 and we are returning after the Christmas break. Our office in Islington has just been refurbished and we can still smell the new paint...

It's important to use positive language, to create a picture your unconscious mind can work towards even when you're not thinking about it. The human brain cannot process a negative – if I ask you not to think of a blue tree, the only way you can do that is to think of one first! Your unconscious mind will hold the internal representation of a blue tree – that is not what you want. So rather than saying 'we no longer wear suits to work', say 'pretty much everyone now comes to work in jeans'.

3.4. What it can do

After our big decision at Bolt Burdon to focus on clients who were willing to pay for exceptional service (in response to the so-called Tesco Law), our management team went away for a couple of days. We took time to envisage our dream future. By taking the time to think about how we wanted our firm to be in ten years, we made many important realisations. But one of them was completely unexpected.

It became crystal clear that we had to move premises. Our building at the time was three terraced properties knocked together, something of a rabbit warren, and we realised it could never reflect the firm we wanted to be – modern, innovative, punching way above its weight and offering an exceptional client experience. Our vision included huge open-plan workspaces, with spaces for chatting, and quiet areas. We envisioned a ground floor where all the walls could be removed for great parties.

We started looking for new premises immediately, and just over a year later, we moved into our beautiful new building. Until we did the visualisation exercise, an office move had not even been on our agenda. As luck would have it, we moved just before the 2008 credit crunch. Thank goodness we did! If we'd left it even a few more months, we may not have had the courage to make the move. The building stretched us financially for the next few years as we strived to grow into it, but never once did we regret it. Our building made a big statement of the firm we wanted to be – it was hugely aspirational and inspirational, just like our vision!

I'm not saying it's impossible to manage a business without a great vision. It's just a lot harder. Without a clear vision, you'll get pulled from pillar to post. You won't know which opportunities to pursue and which to let slip by. If you don't know where you're going, how can you possibly ask anyone to follow you? If you don't know where you're trying to get to, how will you put plans in place? How can you know what you need to do and what your priorities are? If you don't have a clear vision of what success looks like, how will you be inspired to do your best work?

There are so many great payoffs from a clear and compelling vision. A clear vision will help you from being pushed off track. A clear vision will help in decision making. If you know where you're trying to get to, you'll easily be able to make choices in alignment with your core ideology. The vision may help identify priorities. Which is more important: starting that new department or having an office refit? The answer is the one that will help you move towards your vision fastest.

A clear vision of the future will also help people accept an imperfect present. Right now, as I write this, parts of our offices are in need of refurbishment. People are being asked to work at mismatched desks on a carpet that's heading to threadbare in places. But somehow that doesn't feel so bad when everyone knows that this isn't how we want it to be; we're striving to get that refit of lovely, modern, adjustable desks and that bright orange carpet.

A clear vision will help you attract staff who share it. You'll be able to answer the question candidates so frequently ask in interviews, 'Can you tell me a bit about what the plans are for the firm in the future?' It will attract people who are motivated by the vision and, hopefully, put off any that are not.

I believe that establishing a clear and compelling vision is a leader's most important job after making sure the core ideology and strategy are clear. It's not something to be done alone, but it is the leader's job to make sure it's done.

A few great questions

1. Can you see right now, in your mind's eye, a picture of your business ten years from now? A picture that evokes emotion – that makes you want to be there? If not, time to get visioning!

2. Is your vision articulated in detail, so that it can be shared and be motivating to all? Does it include specific examples, such as what people are actually saying, to bring it to life? Is it passionate and emotional? Does it make you want to jump out of bed in the morning?

3. Does your organisation have a single overriding goal or mission? Spend some time thinking about whether one could be found.

RULE 4:
This is how we do things around here!

A code of values exists for every individual, every family and indeed for every group of people who meet regularly. Similarly, every business has a 'how we do things around here' code, whether explicit or not. It's the 'cult' in culture. Most businesses try to make their most important values explicit, but often it's a case of just hanging around for a while to learn how things are done.

Values are just choices – choices about how we're going to live our lives; things like '*it's important to work hard*', and '*always tell the truth*'. We rarely think about them consciously; in fact, for most of us, our values were just picked up from our parents, teachers and peers.

Organisations have values too. Some values are absolute – red lines that can never be crossed, such as instantly dismissing anyone who is dishonest, and some may seem insignificant but still guide our daily lives in the business, like always serving clients fresh coffee, not instant. Values are the rules – written and unwritten – about how we behave towards each other, our clients, our suppliers and the wider community. There will be hundreds of them. Some will apply to the whole organisation and some to a particular department or team.

These organisational values are simply a mixture of the personal values of all the people who work and have worked in the business – starting, of course, with the founders, and then being influenced by all the others who come to be important in it.

4.1. Values

I think there are four types of values in any organisation:

- Core values – reflecting the founders' intent

- Society values – those that most decent people share

- Current organisational values – the ones we're living by right now in our business

- Aspirational values – values we're working towards upholding

4.1.1. Core values

You may have noticed that, somewhat unconventionally, I've chosen to put this Rule about values after the one about vision. This is because any visioning exercise will be done with the core values intact – it would be impossible not to, if they are truly core values.

As I discussed in Rule 1, the founders fixed the 'core ideology' – the core purpose and the core values that are integral to the very existence of the firm. The core ideology will never change. The core values are so fundamental that you'd rather shut up shop than let them go; together with the core purpose, they are the very essence of why the organisation exists.

At the heart of our business are values based on:

- Clients, giving them the very best we can – excellent practical legal advice with the highest ethical standards and amazing service; and

- Staff, creating a great place to work where everyone can learn, flourish and have fun innovating together to build something great.

Core values will not be very specific. They can't be – they will never change, so they need to have room to embrace a changing world.

4.1.2. Society values

Society values are the ones almost everyone shares in our part of the world. There are lots of things we'd all regard as important, such as fairness, telling the truth and treating people with respect. It is not necessary for a business to embrace these society values but it might be hard to attract clients if you do not – it is hard to imagine anyone instructing a law firm that they did not think was honest.

Society values do change. If you have any doubt about that, think about how our society values have changed over the years regarding, say, the recycling of rubbish; or consider the journey of the nation in changing the laws and attitude about sexual orientation. These changes didn't just happen. Both were brought about by a group of people challenging existing values and persuading the nation to change them. A business that embraces a changing society value may be able to leverage this as a point of differentiation from competitors. Do you go further – is it part of your purpose to change an existing society value? Many law firms will be able to claim this in their chosen areas. Or are you leaders in changing a society value, e.g. encouraging your male staff to share parental leave?

4.1.3. Current organisational values

These are the values we live by today in our organisation. Organisational values change just as society values do. The core values are never lost, but others will come and go according to business needs and the values of the individuals working there at any time.

It was only as my firm grew that I began to realise the importance of everyone taking their administrative and management responsibilities seriously. This soon became an explicit value of ours, and one we now regard as so important that we use as it as a performance measure.

Somewhere along the way, we made explicit the value of *'firm first'* – meaning the firm is more important than any individual or any team within the business. Perhaps on reflection *'firm second'* would have been more accurate, because of course clients' best interests always come first. Decisions are made by giving priority to the best interests of the firm as a whole. If necessary, we expect individuals or teams to 'fall on the sword' where this is for the greater good of the firm.

More recently, I was chatting to one of my partners and realised we had another new value. We'd just had a bad experience with a senior person resigning. She'd told us that she was going to take some time out – a break from legal practice – when in fact she simply had another job lined up and was already talking to her clients about it. Had we known she was going to another firm, we would have made different decisions about her departure (probably including garden leave). We were very angry about this and as we ranted we discussed various ways we could cause trouble for our departed colleague. In the end we decided to do nothing and get on with running our own business. As we reflected, my partner said, 'Lynne, one thing I love about our firm is that we always do the right thing'. I realised that 'doing the right thing' had become a value of ours – no matter how badly someone else behaves, we prefer to do what we think is right. They say revenge is sweet, but we don't think so – life is even sweeter on the moral high ground!

Certain values also fade in importance as the world changes. There was a time when we thought it was essential to wear a smart suit to see a client; not any more. In fact, now our value is simply to dress in a way that our clients would expect; that sometimes means a suit, but more often these days it doesn't!

4.1.4. Aspirational values

The thing about values is that if something is a true value, you'll uphold it all the time; it would be almost unthinkable not to. And this is important: when we talk about values, these are the ones that we already hold; the ones we live by every day. Never describe something as a value if you're not already living it, because every time you fail to live up to it, the cynics in the organisation will have a field day. You can imagine the chat around the kettle: 'Ha, they say that, but they don't mean it – look at what happened yesterday…' However, as I said, organisational values change, and can change quite quickly if there's a strong group of people willing to promote the cause.

Thinking about changing values is an important part of the visioning process. Once you have a clear and compelling vision, you'll be able to ask yourself whether you need to let go of any of your current values, and what new values would make that vision a reality; these may become your aspirational values – those you're working towards. By expressing them as aspirational, you silence the cynics – it's much easier to say you're all working towards something than defending a value you don't truly hold. We're working on one at Bolt Burdon now: '*If we say it, we do it!*' At an individual level, this means being reliable, dependable and not making promises we can't deliver. 'No need to chase me. If I said I will do it, I will, no matter what it takes!' At the top team level, it means we'll be increasingly intolerant of those who don't deliver on their obligations and promises.

If something is not already a value, consider carefully whether it's important enough to become an aspirational value. Don't make this decision lightly – creating a new value is a big challenge. But if it's important, it is worth the effort, and there's no better way of making progress towards your vision.

4.2. Define your organisational values

Getting clarity on values is a regular job for the top team. As with the vision, values are probably best revisited every few years. Doing this isn't hard, and it's fun. It's the stuff of away-days. This is an exercise where I feel that a good facilitator is essential, so that everyone can fully participate. As with visioning exercises, it may be good to invite some contributions from rising stars – the partners of the future – as well as the current partners.

4.2.1. Clarify your core ideology

First, make sure your core ideology is crystal clear. If you're in any doubt about it, this must be tackled first. The way to find the core ideology is to ask the founding partners, if they're still around. If they're not, then the current partners will have to ask themselves what they think it is. Ask the direct question, 'What do we think was in the hearts of the founders when they started this business?' If there is a core ideology, it will be visible. If that question yields nothing, then it comes down to you; this time, ask 'What do we want our core purpose and values to be now?' Think about the things you're living now, which you never want to change.

4.2.2. Identify and name your values

Once the core ideology is clear, ask 'What else is important to us around here?' This is a very simple question that's likely to have a huge answer!

There are many ways to do this. The way I do it is to divide the group into small teams of two or three people and ask them to come up with a list of things that are really important – for example, treating everyone in the organisation with equal respect, having lots of social events so that people can get to know each other and celebrating outstanding achievements.

The small teams each identify a list of values, then present them to the group. The job of the whole group is to offer evidence to reinforce a value or to challenge it. Are we really living that value? What evidence is there? Where and how do we infringe it?

Don't get bogged down in the language. This is not a word-crafting exercise (at least not yet). Capture the value in any words that come to mind, and then list as many examples as you can think of where it lives as a value in your organisation – everything you do (and don't do) that demonstrates that value. Then keep refining your definition. What do you really mean? What are you thinking, saying and doing when you're living this value? What are you *not* thinking, saying or doing when you're living this value?

It's likely you'll discover you have many values – too many to remember. As facilitator I might then ask whether some of them are examples of a higher value. For example, are *'give the best legal advice'* and *'serve the best coffee'* both examples of the value *'excellence in everything we choose to do'*?

Make sure each value is expressed at the right level. The value *'delight clients'* is very different from *'satisfy clients'* or *'avoid getting any complaints'*, but each of these could be the value of an organisation. An efficiency business doing routine debt-collection work may be very happy with *'avoid getting any complaints'*, as the service is designed to be as efficient and low priced as possible.

When you've clearly defined your values, name them in a way that is meaningful to you. We know exactly what *'firm first'* means to us. It includes always looking at the bigger picture and putting the long-term best interests of our clients and firm before those of any individual member of staff.

4.3. Hone your definitions

Values that are not properly defined can go astray. We have let that happen in the past, with wanting to be *'a great place to work'*.

Recently, a member of staff resigned. He'd had some poor feedback from a client. In his exit interview, he made a sarcastic remark about how he thought we should care as much about our staff as we did about our clients. We realised our value had gone astray. It was never meant to mean 'a great place to work *for everyone*'. It wasn't meant to be about doing whatever it takes to make everyone happy. It wasn't just about providing great working conditions and having lots of parties and social events. We did want this to be a great place to work, but only for those who did everything possible to try to exceed their clients' expectations. For a while, it had morphed into being nice to everyone who works here and supporting them no matter what – that is not what we meant. We meant we wanted to be a great place to work for those who were dedicated to doing a great job for their clients. We worked on our value definition and gave it greater clarity.

We gave that definition more clarity when we recognised that not everyone wants the same from their place of employment. We want to work with people who want to have fun together, both in and out of the office. This time together outside normal working hours is important. For some people, a great place to work may be a place where you can arrive at 9am, leave at 5pm, and forget all about work again till the next morning. Such a person will not find our environment a happy one.

We got another level of definition after a client complained about one of our solicitors who, according to the client, was not doing a great job. We investigated and took the view that this time it was the client who was being unreasonable. Our solicitor was doing her very best. We terminated the retainer with the client, offering to send all our papers to another firm of his choice and to waive our fee for the work done to date. You can't be a great place to work if you don't support staff when it is right.

A value is truly defined when you build up enough evidence about what it means in practice – when you can say, without question, what you're doing when you live the value, and what you're doing when you don't. And a true value will always have emotion attached to it because it will be so important to you.

4.4. Establish your values hierarchy

Values can often be in conflict. It's therefore helpful to think about their order of importance.

This is easy to do – just take any two of your values and ask, 'If I could only have one of these, which would it be?' So, for example, we have a *'fair management'* value for people who are underperforming, to make sure they have support and every chance to improve. We also have our *'firm first'* value. These two values are sometimes in conflict. We will treat people fairly, and this is often in the firm's best interests: if we can sort the problem, that person will be valuable to us. But where it's clear the issue cannot be sorted, the firm must come first – at the expense of the individual. *'Firm first'* is higher in our values hierarchy. Do this for all the values you've defined, and the values hierarchy will emerge.

We value being 'a great place to work' and 'doing our very best for our clients'. I have spent hours wondering which of these is more important. If I were forced to choose, I would say being a great place to work, because unless we're able to attract the best lawyers, we will not be able to do the best we can for our clients. Our definition of 'best lawyers' means ones who will always want to do their best for their clients. Fortunately, these two values are never in conflict with our clear definitions.

4.5. Know if there are any red lines

Decisions in life are rarely absolute – but sometimes they are! The red lines are the values that you will live by no matter the cost. I am fascinated by absolute beliefs. I went to a Quaker school and I remember talking to my maths teacher about how difficult it was to be a conscientious objector during the war – for him, violence was a red line not to be breached, no matter the cost. I have two vegetarian friends – one will go hungry rather than risk eating something that may contain meat and the other, just every now and then, will accept a bacon sandwich! For one, being a vegetarian is a 'red line'; for the other it's just a choice that can be flexed every now and then.

I think it's helpful to know what your 'red line' values are. So much of life is about making compromises, it isn't very often about absolutes, and so it is good to know where your red lines are.

We have an annual trainee recruitment process. One summer we were recruiting new trainee solicitors to start their training in the following September i.e. in over a year's time. None of the applicants measured up to our standards and we made no appointment at the time. A short while after informing all the applicants that they had not been successful, a new trainee who we'd recruited over a year earlier started work. One of our more recent interviewees learnt of our new starter and accused us of race discrimination – she felt sure that we had preferred a white candidate over her. It was simply not true – she thought the white person who was just starting work was selected in the same process as the one she took part in, which was not the case. She did not accept our explanation and accused us of lying about the process. She engaged lawyers and issued proceedings. When her lawyers heard our side of the story, they suggested that for a small sum of money she would drop her case. This would have been the practical business decision. But we refused. We do not discriminate. We fought the case at considerable cost in our time and legal fees – many hundreds of times the amount we could have paid for the case to be dropped. Of course, we won. For us, this was a matter of principle on which we were not prepared to compromise. We were not prepared to risk any possibility of the world finding out we had settled a race discrimination claim. I know we did the right thing in not compromising that race discrimination case – it felt right, and I could sleep at night with my reputation intact.

A year or two later, we discovered we had a thief in the firm. Cash was being stolen from the coat pockets of members of staff. I discussed it with a select few top-level people and a suggestion was made that we provide lockers for all staff. I think honesty has to be a red-line value of any law firm – clients are trusting us with their money and their information – so we took a different route. We hired a private detective and installed a secret camera in the cloakroom, which was wired to a video recorder hidden under my desk. After hours of viewing videos after all the staff had gone home, the thief was found and dismissed. We knew we could not live with a thief in the firm. We now employ nearly 200 people, and we don't have anything that needs locking in staff areas. If we were to have another thief, better we find out as soon as possible and deal with it.

Another of our core red-line values is to *'uphold the highest standards of professional ethics'*. Not *a high* standard but *the highest* standard. The clients' best interests must always come first. This was tested a couple of years ago. We received a letter on a probate file that was completed many years earlier and the file was in storage. A solicitor got the file out to deal with the query. However, in checking the file he discovered a mistake had been made – the estate had been wrongly distributed and that too much money had been paid to one beneficiary at the expense of the others. In view of the time that had passed since the matter was concluded there was close to zero chance of anyone ever being any the wiser. It was highly unlikely that we would be able to recover the overpayments from any other beneficiary. To confess this mistake was likely to cost us at least £25,000, the excess on our professional indemnity policy. Should we just put this file back in storage and get on with something else? This was not a difficult decision – we always put the client's best interests first. I instructed the solicitor to reopen the file, write to the client and report the matter to our insurers. Any other course of action would have made me feel very bad; even worse, it would have given a message to the solicitor who found the mistake about the true values of our firm.

So how do you know when you are crossing your red line? For me, the answer lies in a feeling – and from the feeling, you can get clear about where your red line is. I knew I did not want to compromise that race discrimination claim or install staff lockers. It would have just felt wrong! When you know where your red lines are, difficult decisions become much easier. Compromise becomes easier too – you know where you can compromise, and you know where you simply cannot.

4.6. Pay the price

Living your values is not always easy. Doing your best for a client may mean delivering some advice that the client doesn't want to hear, or it may mean sacrificing time with the family at the weekend to do some urgent work that the client needs first thing Monday.

Living *'firm first'* will mean being intolerant of anyone who doesn't share this belief. That can be very hard. You've hired a new recruit, they're performing well and hitting all their financial targets, making money for you. They pay lip-service to the idea of *'firm first'* and say all the right things in meetings. It's only after a year or two that you notice their client-hoarding, their reluctance to share marketing initiatives, and you realise their true value is *'me first'*. If *'firm first'* is a true value for your organisation, that person must be challenged, confronted, and probably managed out. The short-term benefits of their excellent performance will never be worth the long-term damage to the firm you want to build.

Incidentally, I do believe everyone should prioritise their own self-interest – as I like to say 'put yourself at the centre of your life'. *'Firm first'* means assembling a group of individuals who all truly believe they'll thrive best in an organisation that upholds this value.

4.7. Reap the reward

Except for founders, there'll rarely be a perfect match between personal and organisational values. What is important is an alignment of values – meaning that for each individual's most important values about work, there is a connection, not a conflict, with the values of the business. If the business has a clearly stated set of values, any individual will know immediately if they might be happy working there. Even when a person has not given any particular thought to their own values, they'll be aware of them unconsciously. No one is going to be happy working for a firm whose values are not in alignment with their own. If an individual's values are not in alignment with those of the organisation, they'll live in fear of being judged or rejected. It will only be a matter of time before they go and look for another organisation more suited to them. Without a clear set of values – a clear message on 'how we do things around here' – everything will be harder. It will take longer for individuals to work out if there's alignment between their personal values and the business values.

But when there's synergy between the values of the organisation and those of everyone who works in it, everyone will get a strong feeling of belonging – of being part of the same tribe – and that feels good. Those lovely brain chemicals that make us feel safe and content will be released, and we'll instinctively want to work with team spirit.

The other big benefit of having a clearly defined set of values, ranked in order of importance, is in decision making. Law firm mergers abound; we've considered a few, but for us it's often been a short conversation, with no need to even look at the figures. If the values don't fit, it'll be too hard to make it work. With clearly defined values, it's easy to decide between options, and once a decision is made it will be unshakable, because you'll know why you made it. Compromise also becomes easier because you're clear on what you can and can't give up on, and you know where the lines are drawn.

This approach will not just work for you and your staff but for clients too, and indeed all the other stakeholders. If everyone knows what the firm stands for, they'll easily be able to decide whether it's the right firm for them.

A few great questions

1. Are you clear about your own personal values?

2. Are you clear about the core values of your business – the ones that will never change?

3. Are there any 'society values' that you are campaigning to change or that you are actively embracing?

4. Are you clear about your current business values – the ones you are truly living? If not, what are you going to do about it?

5. Are there any special values for your team or different parts of the organisation?

6. Where are your 'red lines' – the values that are absolute with no space for compromise?

7. What is the price you're paying for your values – and what are the payoffs?

Rule 5:
Always make a plan!

The business plan is the road map for getting from where you are now to your envisioned future by taking a route in alignment with your values.

The plan identifies what you're going to do – and in which order. Alongside the plan sits the budget, which is the costing of the plan and an estimate of income that will arise as a result of implementing the plan. A clear business plan is an essential document for every organisation.

5.1. My business plan journey

I wrote my first business plan in 1985. We were in the midst of our horrible partnership dispute and we were planning the start of Bolt Burdon. We'd found a building – a four-storey freehold terrace building in the middle of Islington, which had been a newsagent with flat above. We needed to borrow money to buy the building and fund the start of our new business. I phoned a bank manager – Peter, whom I'd dealt with a few times for a client – and he said he'd see us in a few days and that I should bring our business plan with me. I had no idea what one of those was. But I decided to apply common sense and put together a plan that included who we expected our clients to be, what we expected to bill in the first year of trading, and the expenses we expected to pay in the first year. I also made a list of property acquisition costs and the equipment we'd need to buy. We asked for a mortgage on the building (£60,000), a bridging loan pending the sale of my flat (£25,000), a five-year loan to purchase equipment (£20,000 – including £7,000 for a word processor, £150 for an 'adding machine' and £2,500 for a telex machine!) and a £10,000 overdraft on the office account.

Whilst we were waiting for the day of our appointment to arrive, things had heated up considerably on the purchase of our building and we found ourselves in a contracts race.

I'll never forget the day of that meeting. We were shown up a grand, winding staircase at the back of the banking hall on the Strand, and through a secret door half-way up the first flight of stairs to Peter's huge office. We chatted for half an hour about our plans, and then he said, 'Yes, okay then'. 'You mean we can have the money we need?' I said – 'The mortgage, the five-year loan, the bridging loan and the overdraft?' 'Yes,' he replied. 'Can I rely on that?' I asked. He was getting a bit fed up now. '*Yes!* Of course, there will be paperwork, but you can rely on it.' I asked if I could use his phone. He was now very surprised, but didn't seem to mind, so I picked up the phone on his desk and exchanged contracts on the purchase of our building there and then. In that half hour, our new firm became a reality! That first business plan was enough to make our dream come true. Peter told us a couple of years later he'd dined out on that story a few times!

We've prepared a business plan and budget every year since then. Our plans have become increasingly sophisticated as I've learnt more about running a business.

5.2. Why the plan is important

There are several important reasons for writing a business plan.

The discipline of a written plan forces you to think about what you actually need to do, and in which order. It forces you to decide what the next steps are going to be to move you towards your vision. It also becomes a great tool for communication with your staff and other stakeholders. A good plan for the year will help you as you plan your own time. As you plan each week and each day, it will be clear where you must spend your time, who you need to talk to and where to spend your resources.

Perhaps most importantly, in times of stress, a plan will remind you what you decided when you were thinking calmly and strategically. We all know those moments when you can't think, when you can't sleep, when you're literally 'worried sick' or completely overwhelmed. When we're under threat of any sort, our most basic human need is to stay safe. Our brain will prioritise this above everything. The more ancient parts of our brain will take over and instruct us simply to follow what's worked before – but that is unlikely to be the new behaviour you've prioritised in your plan! The part of our brain that evolved more recently – the part that endows us with strategic reasoning (our 'human brain') – will be held offline until we feel safe and able to cope with change again.

Preparing the annual business plan takes months, not days. The process should be started long before the beginning of the year of the plan. My plans have always been for a financial year – from April to March. I like to start my thinking over the Christmas break – a happy pastime for those long December days.

5.3. Before you start

Before thinking about what you're going to do, you need to think about what's happening in the world around you. Any plan must be written in the context of the external environment. This may be the most important part of the business-planning process. Invest time in taking a long, hard look at the world you're going to operate in.

Ask some questions:

- What are the global trends you need to take into account?

- What are Generations Y and Z expecting from their workplace?

- Are there going to be any legal changes that affect you? Might there be a general election and a change of government? What might that mean for your business?

- Is there any research you can do – e.g. about your target markets?

- Why not ask your key clients what's important to them right now?

- What about your competitors? At the very least, have a look at their websites, and those of your clients.

- Is there any benchmarking information you'd find useful, e.g. about your competitors? There are lots of good benchmarking surveys that law firms can buy.

Next, make an honest assessment of where you are now. I still love the good old SWOT analysis: four lists of your current strengths, weaknesses, opportunities and threats. You'll need some statistics too. Which teams are profitable? Where are you losing money, and are you going backwards or forwards in resolving that? You can ask whether your current structure is serving you – or do you have some efficiency work that you're treating as experience work? And listen to your gut – who are your best people and why? Who is not performing and why? The brutal truth is needed here.

5.4. Writing the plan

Making the business plan is the job of all the top team, with input from a wide range of others in the firm too. The leader needs to make sure it's done, but it is a team sport – it's really important to get input from as many people as possible and to consider as much relevant external information as you can find. Making the plan will need two or three months to allow for all the necessary meetings.

A good annual plan has three sections: a review of the last year (a summary of the highlights and achievements and a note of any goals that were not met and need more work); the long-term plan (this describes your core ideology and vision, and long-term goals for the next five years or more); and the plan for the next 12 months (which identifies the priorities and goals for the year ahead).

5.4.1. Section 1: Review of the year just gone

I first introduced a review of last year in our business plans because it was a requirement of one of our quality standards. At the time, I was not convinced it was helpful. But as I've begun to understand more about people and how our brains work, I've become increasingly converted to the importance of this. A review of last year will provide evidence to the reader that plans work. Our brains are pattern-recognition machines.[10] Our unconscious mind looks for patterns, and where it sees something working, it remembers that. By reviewing last year's plan and demonstrating that following the plan resulted in success, we give confidence that this year's plan is likely to work too. If there were things we didn't achieve, we can examine the reasons for that and either resolve to address them in this year's plan or decide to abandon them and move on to more effective things.

The plan is also a place where we can recognise individual successes – a great case win, or a very successful team. Public recognition makes people feel good.

Although this section will come first in the final plan, it can probably only be written in outline for the first draft – there will still be a month or two of the old year left.

5.4.2. Section 2: The long-term plan

Restating the most important things

This part of the plan will not change much from year to year. However, it is very important when you remember who will read the plan. I believe the plan (though not the budget) should be freely available to all staff and other key stakeholders. It is especially helpful for new members of staff, to give them an insight into the business they've joined.

That's why I believe it's essential that the long-term plan starts with a statement of: core ideology (why the firm exists – core purpose and core values); highest-level strategy (the sort of work we do and clients we serve); vision (where we are going); values (how we behave).

Then it can go on to specify our goals and priorities for long-term change. There's a big difference between the vision (a dream, how it could be if everything goes the best it can) and a decision to achieve a specific goal within a specified time.

Long-term goals

I am a great believer in setting goals. Back to the brain science again: when we set a clear goal, this stimulates the release of dopamine and that will motivate us to act.

I think it's important to consider two types of goal – 'outcome goals' (specific outcomes e.g. turnover target) and 'process goals' (specific regular behaviours, such as everyone doing their billing regularly). Both are important. A process goal may lead towards an outcome goal or it may just be a desired behaviour.

Outcome goals must be SMART. There are lots of interpretations of this well-known acronym; my favourite is Specific, Measurable, Achievable, Relevant and Timed, and the most important of these is Timed. The thing about a SMART goal is there must be a day in the future where you can ask the question: has this goal been achieved or not? A goal to 'send clients invoices more regularly' is not SMART. A goal to 'reduce the average time taken between doing work and invoicing clients to 60 days by the last day of the financial year' is SMART.

Process goals are important too. To achieve the SMART goal mentioned previously, behaviours will have to change, and so a process goal of, say, 'every Friday, each team leader must confirm to the finance manager that all appropriate invoices have been sent to clients' might work. This is a behaviour upon which managers can hold their staff to account.

Long-term goals also need to have milestones. A goal to increase realisation ratio (a measure of rate charged per hour against a target rate) from 80% to 90% over five years may have milestones of a 2% increase each year. Each year there may be different things to tackle to work towards this goal, such as tighter procedures for client acceptance to make sure all clients are in the target market, tighter controls at billing time, perhaps a second pair of eyes to consider if the right amount is being billed, a marketing campaign to attract work that can command higher fees…

Things you need to consider

When thinking about what you want to include in the plan, always remember that all law firms compete in two markets: the competition for talent and the competition for clients. I always start with these two questions:

- What more can we do to attract and retain the very best people? Think about the things that are important to them – great training, flexible working, good benefits, etc.

- What can we do to attract and retain more of the best clients? Think about what makes our services more attractive to them – lawyer availability and accessibility, relevant legal news updates, etc.

Next I think about the big structural aspects of the business, for example:

- Is it necessary to address legal structure or governance? There are a number of choices now: limited company, LLP or traditional partnership. Which serves our strategy the best?

- Do we need to address internal structure? Do we have our leverage (ratio of partners to other staff) right for the type of work we do? Are our teams or work groups of the right size so that people can feel a good sense of belonging to 'family-size' teams?

Financial goals are always going to be an important part of any plan. Some of these will be specifically mentioned in the long-term plan, many more will be implicit in the budget. Incidentally, the budget also needs to be in two parts – long-term in outline and short-term in detail. Never forget that a business needs to make a profit and have healthy cash flow. If not, the entire business will be under threat! What are your most important financial measures and where do you need to make improvements?

Stephen Mayson describes the key drivers of profit in Chapter 28 of *Making Sense of Law Firms*.[11] There are only five things that affect profit per partner – easily remembered with his acronym RULES:

- Rates or realisation – a measure of how much is paid for each hour worked

- Utilisation – hours worked on client engagements – usually expressed as a percentage of hours available for client work

- Leverage – the ratio of staff to profit-sharing partners

- Expenses – the costs of running the business

- Speed – the speed at which work done can be turned into cash – usually measured in days and split into the time from doing the work to billing it, known as 'work-in-progress (WIP) days' and the time from billing to cash collection, known as 'debtor days'; together known as 'lockup'.

It is important to think carefully about each of these factors. What is the target level for each of them for your firm?

I believe you should always start with utilisation. If utilisation is low this can only mean one of three things: lawyers don't have enough work; or they're not recording time properly; or they're lazy (almost never true in my experience). If utilisation is low, this must be fixed first. But it's a one-off fix. We want our lawyers to work at 100% utilisation, but not more than that, as more means other things may be neglected or may lead to burnout or other health issues. If we have people who have utilisation that is not in the range of 95% to 105% we must address this first.

The right leverage will depend on the work being done. High volume, low cost efficiency work will need higher leverage than very complicated expertise work.

Expenses need to be planned thoughtfully – low is not necessarily better. Are you investing enough in IT to ensure your competitiveness for the future? Are you overspending unnecessarily, e.g. by paying for temporary staff because of problems with your recruitment strategy?

Speed is often a big problem for law firms – consider what you can do this year to improve lockup. There is no one size fits all answer to what is the right level of lockup – it will depend on the work you do but you should always be looking for improvements.

And finally rates or realisation. There is potentially no limit on the amount you can charge if you are able to increase the added value for your clients. A specific improvement in hourly rates achieved or realisation ratio would always be a great SMART goal.

Consider your infrastructure and back office systems – the people, policies and procedures to manage HR, compliance, IT, finance and support teams. Do you need to make changes so that these best serve the business? Time and time again, I've learnt how important infrastructure is. I now absolutely believe that any successful business should have the best infrastructure it can afford. In my experience, many lawyers are not very interested in infrastructure or systems – but I don't think this is optional for the leader. A managing partner can engage the very best professional managers but they must accept that they are responsible for infrastructure and they must know enough to be sure the firm's systems are robust and fit for purpose. The tasks can be delegated, but ultimate responsibility cannot.

Probably the most important part of the infrastructure is IT – without great technology, a business just cannot be competitive. Law firms in particular need a lot of specialist IT for case management and looking after client money. These systems are incredibly expensive to buy and maintain. Lawyers now expect to be able to work anywhere in the world just as if they were at their desk in the office. Cybercrime is rife – client data and business continuity must be protected.

Compliance has now become a respected profession. Regulation is very demanding – it cannot be ignored. We must follow the rules of the Solicitors Regulation Authority, have financial audits, consider money-laundering regulations, comply with data laws... the list is endless. We must make sure we protect ourselves from serious disaster with robust business continuity systems. We need expert professional staff and we need robust procedures.

The law firm cash office is an integral part of the business – millions of pounds will pass through the cashiers' hands every day. We need very strong systems to protect our clients' money.

Employing people is increasingly complicated. We must make sure payroll works well and pension schemes are administered. We must follow rules about maternity, sickness, holidays and other leaves of absence. The HR function is critical, not only to make sure we comply with the law but also to make sure our staff are well looked after.

And don't forget the premises – people want to work in an environment that is clean and where the building is opened on time. They want good showers and somewhere to put their stuff.

Think about each of these areas and decide whether any improvements are necessary in the coming years – do you want to set specific goals (e.g. replace the practice management system within the next five years) or just earmark something to be thought about later (e.g. an office refurbishment)? This will reassure your people that you're aware of what needs to be done even if it's not a priority for this year.

5.4.3. Section 3: This year's plan

This part of the plan may not be very long – indeed it's probably better if it's not – but it is important because it will specifically state what you will do and achieve over the next 12 months.

It will include specific goals for the year – either short-term initiatives (e.g. 'In May, our compliance manager will review our social media policy') or a step in a long-term initiative (e.g. 'This year, as part of our long-term initiative to improve our realisation ratio from 80% to 90%, we will improve it to 82%').

It is important to set the goals and to be clear on how you are going to achieve them. Who needs to change what behaviours? It's new behaviours that will bring about the desired short-term changes, which lead to the long-term changes, which lead towards the vision.

I am a great believer in one firm-wide top priority – the one thing that's most important for everyone to work towards. A theme for the year that, if achieved, would push the business more towards the vision than anything else you can think of. This is the thing that as a leader you're going to spend most of your time on – the thing you'll be directing every senior manager towards. Maybe it will be a financial target, e.g. hitting a turnover figure. Maybe it will be working on that aspirational value, e.g. 'If we say it, we do it'. It's very important to get a commitment from all the top team that they will lead by example on this, and that you the leader will hold them all to account on it.

After identifying the top priority, I suggest a handful of other goals. SMART deliverables with clear, allocated responsibilities. These might include an important IT project, a marketing initiative, improving the recruitment procedure, a new staff bonding initiative.

The business plan includes things that are of firm-wide interest. Of course, every team and every individual will have their own set of goals too.

Because the plan will be read by staff and other stakeholders, it's always going to be helpful to explain why the choices have been made. It may also be useful to discuss other options that were considered (for example, why we decided this year to invest in a new team doing a new area of work, rather than refurbish the offices).

5.5. Write the goals on a tablet of stone

Each year, set clear goals and a clear budget for the year. These are what you're going to measure yourself against and once set they do not change.

You will also set out the actions you are going to take to achieve these goals and budget. These may change as things progress during the year. If you find something is not working, then change what you are doing – but the original goal stays fixed. The plan should be reviewed frequently in top team meetings so that nothing gets forgotten and initiatives that are not working can be identified and revised. We have always published to our staff a formal review at the half-way point so that people can see our progress against our goals.

There is no joy in measuring yourself against a moving target. Setting and achieving goals is very rewarding, but your brain will not be fooled if the goalposts change – you will know you were just fooling yourself. This needs discipline. If things start slipping, it's tempting to revise the goals to make them realistic again. But it's much better to keep the goal and acknowledge it's only part met – and that you will be trying again next year!

5.6. The game-changing magic of a good plan

The only way a well-thought-out plan can fail is if you fail to follow it. And if you allow each day to drift by without taking the action you set out in the plan, everyone will know, and everyone will become demoralised.

A well-thought-out plan that is followed, however, will give you confidence that you're progressing towards your vision.

As you make progress against the plan through the year, you will feel good – those happy brain chemicals will be released, making you feel pleased with what you've achieved and motivated to keep going.

Your people will be able to see the progress, too. They'll feel part of a firm that knows where it's going and is taking action to get there.

When the plan is written, it's the leader's job to deliver it, to see that it is followed through and to do whatever it takes to make sure the goals are met. Of course, you won't do this alone, but you must take responsibility for managing others – persuading, cajoling, instructing, holding to account so that the plan gets delivered.

A few great questions

1. Think about a SWOT analysis: strengths, weaknesses, opportunities and threats. This doesn't need a grand away-day (although that would be best); right now, try a coffee and the back of an envelope. Pay particular attention to opportunities and threats; these often come from the same external conditions. Are there any things you have previously missed?

2. Why not spend a happy hour cruising around the websites of your competitors to see what they're up to?

3. Will you invest in a benchmarking survey to see how you're performing against your competitors?

4. Invite some of your rising stars to dinner – ask them what they'd like to see in the next plan – make it clear that you're looking for ideas now, and will make decisions later.

5. Do you have one priority for the year? One thing that will make your firm a better one a year from now? One thing that – come hell or high water – you're going to make sure you deliver?

6. Are you sure everyone in your organisation knows your core ideology, strategy, vision, values and priorities for long-term change? Use your annual plan to state these every year.

7. Do you have clear long-term and short-term goals – with budgets? Is there one clear priority – the thing that is most important – the thing you will tackle first each day?

Rule 6:
Good communication is mission-critical!

People feel safe when they think they're in the right tribe. But they can't know that unless they know what the firm stands for. There's no point in having spent time articulating your core ideology, strategy, vision, values and short- and long-term plans unless you then communicate all this information clearly to your team.

Listening is important too. In a happy family, everyone is important – everyone is listened to. And so it is in a law firm – everyone wants to feel their voice is heard.

6.1. I learnt the hard way

When Roger and I started Bolt Burdon, communication was easy. There were just five of us, and we worked closely together. I was able to tell everyone what was going on. We were all friends – a little work family. Within five years, we'd grown from five to 20 people. We'd begun to develop a team structure, with each team doing a distinct area of work. We appointed some lateral hires who didn't understand our culture (we probably didn't understand it ourselves at that point, and we'd certainly never explained it to anyone). We knew things were not right, so we appointed a management consultant called Harry, who did some research for us.

He spoke to our clients, and found we excelled at communicating with them. Their comments included:

> *'Service is always excellent. The partners are accessible and they return calls promptly. They are more expensive than average, but we know we get a quality service.'*

> *'We get excellent service from Bolt Burdon in terms of access to partners and being kept informed. We also use another firm of solicitors, but place more complicated work with Bolt Burdon.'*

> *'The partners at Bolt Burdon are very direct. They get the job done without wasting time.'*

Unfortunately, our staff did not feel the same. Harry reported morale was very low. Comments fed back to us included:

'There has been a loss of personal communication as the firm has grown.'

'The partners keep having these meetings, but they say one thing and do another.'

'The communication structure needs to be improved. We always feel we're in the dark. There is no system of regular communication from the top downwards.'

'At appraisals they ask you what you think, but that's as far as it goes.'

'When it comes to personal problems, they're very good at listening to you and helping; but communication within the firm is a real problem.'

I was really upset. Creating a good working environment was so important to us. I realised that I had been so focused on looking after clients that I had neglected the happiness of our staff. I desperately wanted to get this right – I felt I had let everyone down.

Harry also discovered another mistake. Our firm was profitable from day one but because we were growing so fast we never had enough cash in the bank. Sometimes we had to go to the Legal Aid Board to ask for extra money for work we had done under the 'hardship' rule. Roger and I were always confident we would find the money we needed to pay the salaries somehow – and we always did. But as we felt it was best to foster a culture of honesty and openness, we were always frank with our staff about this. What we didn't realise was that we were scaring people. Because we always seemed to be worrying about cash, people were nervous about the future of the firm. Harry told us we were 'sharing information with people whose shoulders were not broad enough to bear it'.

Those words have stuck with me forever. It's the partners who are paid to bear the responsibility of paying the salaries. Our staff simply needed to know their salaries would always be paid.

I don't think we're alone in making these mistakes. Over the last 30 years I've interviewed hundreds of people who want to come and work for us. One of my favourite questions to ask them is 'If you woke up tomorrow morning and found you'd suddenly become managing partner of your current firm, what's the first thing you would change?' About 80% of the replies are about improving communication!

I hear things like:

> *'The partners are very secretive – no one knows what's going on'*

> *'There doesn't seem to be any plan at all'*

> *'People are leaving but no one knows why'*

> *'I'm worried the firm is not doing well financially'*

Communication is a tricky business, and you need to invest time in making sure you get it right.

You must communicate with all your staff, stakeholders, clients, suppliers and the wider community; they are all interested, to some degree, in your plans. But by far the most important are your people. It is communication with those who work in the organisation that I'm going to address in this Rule.

Remember: people need to know what the organisation stands for, and where it's going – so that they know they're in the right tribe. They also want to know they have strong leaders with broad shoulders who will keep them safe when the going gets tough.

6.2. Top-down communication

The most important communication is making sure everyone understands the core ideology, the vision, the values, the long-term goals and what the firm is going to do this year. This is the job of the leader and the top team and, fortunately, it's relatively straightforward. It's not enough to email the business plan to everyone! The leader needs to speak often – and always with the same clear, consistent and compelling message.

If you can get your whole organisation in a single room, I recommend the managing partner makes an annual presentation to the firm. However, once a year is definitely not enough. It's impossible to over-communicate the key messages. It is the job of the leader and the top team to reinforce this message at every possible opportunity. It is constant repetition that lets people know you're serious about the message and how important it is to you.

Every time there's a meeting at any level in the organisation, find a way to restate part of your plan. It's easy to do – start the meeting by stating why the discussion is important, and this will always take you back to your core ideology or vision.

Make sure you – the leader – get to meet new recruits at some point during their induction so that you can tell them face to face about the core ideology, vision and values. I have always believed this is one of the managing partner's most important meetings. This is where you can set the tone for a long-term relationship of openness. Where you can let people know that you want to hear what they have to say and that you encourage questions. Make it clear that you love talking about the firm and that there are very few issues you're not happy to talk about openly.

Internal training sessions are another good way to communicate the organisational values. In fact, I would say this is one of the main advantages of organising in-house training.

When I am delivering training I never miss a chance to explain why we exist and what is important to us. Sometimes I wonder if people are saying 'Here comes Lynne – stand by for vision and values!'

6.3. A two-way process

Listening is just as important as talking. Remember the adage: we were given two ears and one mouth for a reason. You must listen all the time, and especially listen to your staff. The higher you get in a business, the further you get from the coal face. Make sure you create opportunities to talk to your people. You have to create these – very few people will feel confident enough to invite the managing partner for lunch!

Lunch is a great way to listen – and I don't leave it to chance. Whenever someone has lunch with me they can expect my favourite question. 'If you were managing partner in this firm, what's the first thing you'd change?'

Shorter chats are just as valuable – eating together around the kitchen table, or on the firm walk or at evening drinks. The leader needs a store of good questions – maybe 'What is the best thing that happened to you at work today?' 'How are you feeling about your work?' 'Where do you see your career five years from now?' 'Who do you really enjoy working with?'

But be careful – if you are seeking views on something specific, e.g. 'How do you feel about our training programme?', make it clear that you're listening for views only, and then you will be deciding. Sometimes people mistake a genuine interest in their opinion as a signal that they are going to help make the decision. Law firms are not democracies – ultimately the top team must decide and accept the responsibility for their decisions. But if you can find small ways to let people know they're being heard, then do so – someone saying at the kitchen table how short of cash they are at the end of the month might really appreciate a quiet word in private later, offering a salary advance. If you get a suggestion with an easy quick fix – do it!

6.4. Face to face is always best

Sooner or later, the 'anonymous suggestion box' will be raised. It's a personal view, but I'm not really interested in the opinion of anyone who isn't prepared to put their name to it. I want to be able to explore the suggestion, and there's nothing as effective for that as face-to-face communication. Albert Mehrabian discovered that, when talking about feelings and attitudes (which would include core ideology, vision and values), the words you use constitute only about 7% of face-to-face communication. Body language constitutes 55%, and voice and tone 38%.[12] This explains why face-to-face communication is so important if you want to get your message across with passion and emotion. It's why email is so difficult – it's very hard to convey feelings with just words. Telephone is a bit better, but we still miss out on 55% of the possible depth of communication.

Of course, it's critical that you tell the truth! If your body language does not support your words (and it's very difficult to control your body language) then you're in trouble. We humans are adept at deducing what someone is saying by body language and tone of voice; if these don't match up with the words being spoken, we will tend to believe the body language. There are two problems then – you will not get the current message across and, worse, your own credibility will be damaged.

Do not shy away from problems – people want their leaders to lead. This is especially true in difficult times. When the business is facing a problem, it's no good pretending it doesn't exist – that will just fire up the rumour mill. People are not stupid and will nearly always be aware a problem exists. Our brains are wired to look for danger – all day, every day. If there are any signs of trouble (the managing partner sitting at his desk with his head in his hands, or suddenly a lot of visits from the bank manager), people will assume the worst. People need a lot of reassurance. If there's no problem (maybe that managing partner had a personal problem or was just doing some serious thinking), then it's important to keep saying everything is going well. Even better, if you're meeting the bank manager to explore a loan for some exciting new kit, why not say so! But if there's a problem, there's no point ignoring it; and if you don't acknowledge it, speculation will be rife.

As soon as there's any doubt about the health of the firm, people will begin to feel threatened, and that's when the trouble in the kitchen starts. Yes – the most successful communication in a law firm happens in the kitchen, while waiting for the kettle to boil! It just takes one person who is feeling insecure to ask a colleague 'Do you think they're going to make redundancies?' and before you know it, the rumour mill is at work. Kettle rumours are the most infectious I know – but unfortunately, they only seem to work for bad news, and often such 'news' isn't even true. What this means is that if you're not very careful to over-communicate your message, the people who have the most influence in the firm will be those who spend the most time in the kitchen!

If there really is a problem, then good communication is more important than ever. What people need, to make them feel safe, is an acknowledgement of the problem and reassurance from the leaders that they know what to do about it, and that progress is being made towards the solution.

Of course, it's often not possible or wise to recount the full extent of a problem. Remember what Harry said about shoulders that are broad enough to bear it. You'll need to think carefully about what exactly to say.

I think I got it right when we had to make our first ever redundancies. We had known for many years that the number of legal secretaries we needed would reduce – technology was moving on apace and we were committed to investing in the best available. For years I had stated this was inevitable in our business plans but also I said that we'd be able to reduce numbers by secretaries naturally moving on, and we didn't expect to make redundancies. What I hadn't thought through was that all other law firms would be doing the same. The result was that no secretaries were resigning. Eventually, we had to face that truth.

Cash flow was very difficult as personal injury work switched from being funded by legal aid (where we got interim payments) to 'no win no fee' where there was much less scope for payments before the end of the case. We were left with no choice – we would need to make two secretaries redundant and we had no alternative positions to offer. If cash had not been so tight I'm sure we would have hung on for longer. We were a good team and all our secretaries (about ten of them at the time) were good people. The challenge was to take the necessary action and continue to keep everyone else on board.

I made a presentation to our staff. I explained the effect of the changes and stressed that our business remained sound. I drew a graph showing what had happened to our cash flow so far, over the last four years, and how we'd delivered almost exactly on my projection. I explained carefully what was happening and that we were on track, but that we had to remain very careful. And I announced that after looking at every option, we had reluctantly concluded that we needed to make two secretaries redundant. I could not hold back a few tears. We'd never had to make redundancies before. It was possibly the hardest and most heartfelt speech I had ever had to make. I was honest, sad, strong and confident. Every word I said was true. I am proud of how I handled that. Whilst no one was happy, I do think everyone understood. I didn't get any negative feedback, or indeed any alternative suggestions. I sometimes wonder if some people were thinking *it's about time, too*, as the oversupply of secretaries was apparent to many.

It is at these times that the leader is the most important person. When there are problems to tackle, people want to hear the leader say 'I know we have a problem or a challenge. We've worked out how to solve it. This is what we're going to do, and this is what we need you to do. Let's do it!'

6.5. Everyone hears something different

It's said that we only hear what we want to hear, and to some extent that's true. Because of our life experiences, we all have a unique set of filters governing how we take in information. There is more information coming in to our brain through our senses than we can process so our brains filter that information according to what we're currently focusing on. This means we'll hear the stuff that is important to us, and ignore other things, without even realising it. Have you ever been in a meeting and come out feeling really positive about what was said, only to then meet a colleague who was also there but says to you, 'Wow, that was a meeting of gloom and doom'? Same meeting, different filters.

This is why you must communicate and over-communicate. You must tell your message every which way, and at every possible opportunity so that everyone hears it.

6.6. Walk the talk

Coming from Stockton-on-Tees, I have a reputation for some northern bluntness. I call a spade a spade. I know I sometimes lack tact, but over the years, it's served me well. I do believe that if I say something, our people trust that it's true.

It's so important that as a leader you build trust. You can only do that by making sure you're consistently honest. Remember that because of the way our brain works, people will be watching you carefully – unconsciously – for evidence that you mean what you say. If they get that evidence it will make them feel safe. Trust will be built.

If you do something that contradicts what you say, they will spot it in an instant. So don't say, 'We're short of cash', and then go out and buy a new car. I guarantee someone will notice, and the chat around the kettle will boil up again. Similarly, it's no good putting in the business plan that something is very important unless you, the leader, are enforcing it daily. All communication will be valueless unless it's reinforced by your actions.

The same goes for the top team. Nothing is more damaging to a business than a senior member of staff who, on the face of it, has credibility and is perceived to be 'in the know', but who is not on message with the plan. There are bound to be issues on which not everyone will agree – these are for the privacy of management meetings. There's no place in a law firm for a partner who undermines a decision made. A disgruntled partner or senior member of staff who makes undermining comments to junior people can do untold damage.

By communicating the plan repeatedly and consistently, everyone in the organisation will be crystal clear about what's important and where you're heading.

It is also important that the leader is visible and approachable! Questions directly to the leader need to be encouraged. Beware of shut doors, 'out of office' on permanently – mystery breeds speculation.

Finally, communicate with passion and determination – remember how important the body language is. People want to follow a leader who has the necessary skills, who can be trusted and who has the passion and determination to see the job through.

To make the most of this, make sure you enjoy public speaking. This is just a skill, and can be learnt. I'll never forget the first time I had to speak in public – it was just a Chamber of Commerce lunch and my task was simply to say a very few words at the end of the event to thank the speaker and give the date of the next meeting. I was so terrified I couldn't eat any of the lunch – my stomach was in knots and it was all I could do to push the food around my plate and hope my neighbours would not notice. I knew that I must overcome this fear and I vowed to myself on that day that whenever I was asked to speak in future, I would just say 'Yes'. And I did. I forced myself to speak in public whenever I got the opportunity. I also booked some training and I have honed my skills over the years. Now I can honestly say I love public speaking!

The rewards for making sure everyone understands the core ideology, vision, values and goals are huge. If this is done year after year, month after month, day after day, you will find that everyone is pulling in the same direction. Morale will be high, because everyone feels safe, and everyone believes good progress is being made, and everyone's getting their happy brain chemicals.

A few great questions

1. Why not make a list of all the ways you can think of sharing your message with your people – formally and informally?

2. Are you able to speak with passion? You need to be a confident speaker. If you're not, think about some public speaking training.

3. Are you communicating so much that the chat around the kettle doesn't stand a chance?

4. When did you last have lunch with a junior member of your team – no agenda – just to chew the fat?

Rule 7:
EAGLES only on this bus!

I often say that if there were just one thing I could change over the past 30 years, it would be to get recruitment right more often. I believe this would have made more difference to our profitability than anything else!

I want to start this Rule with what are now my two fundamental recruitment beliefs.

The first is that we must recruit for attitude before skills. Of course we want the necessary skills too but skills can be learnt – attitude comes from values and thus is unlikely to change. We want to find people like us – people who share our values and beliefs. I have known this for a long time, but no one explains why this is important better than Jim Collins in *Good to Great*:[13] where he suggests that getting the right people 'on the bus' is critical to having a great business and further if you don't have the right people 'on the bus' it doesn't matter how good your strategy is – you still won't have a great business.

The second belief is that the recruitment bar must constantly go up. If you want your business to improve, you must constantly raise the bar of recruitment standards. What was acceptable for a recruit last year is not good enough today. The firm *is* its people. Every single recruit is a vote either to make the firm better, or to allow standards to slip a little. We have to be prepared to recruit people who are, or can become, better than we are. If we don't, the firm can never be better than it is now. It means recruitment is one of the most important things you do.

7.1. The recruitment lottery

We were very lucky when we started Bolt Burdon in 1986. A number of colleagues wanted to follow us to our new firm, meaning we were able to choose from some really good people – tried and tested team members who were keen to work for us. We were off to a flying start.

We grew rapidly, and recruiting new staff quickly became a priority. I was soon to learn that recruitment could be a very hit-and-miss affair!

Our first recruit was Annie – our very first word processor operator. (Yes, that was a job in 1986!) We all liked her – she was skilled and fun. But Annie couldn't seem to understand 'urgency'. It didn't seem to click that we couldn't sell our client's flat while we were waiting for her to type a lease, or that every day we delayed finalising the draft of a court claim was one day longer our client had to wait for his compensation. Annie had other priorities. It didn't take me too long to realise that this was my error. I'd failed to make it clear to her that in our firm, if we need to stay late to get a job done, that is what we do.

Keith, on the other hand, was a recruitment success. We had grown considerably, and I'd decided we needed an office junior – someone to change the light bulbs, fill the printers, stuff envelopes, etc. One of the first people I interviewed for this role was Keith. He was only 16, and very nervous in his interview. He'd left school with no GCSEs. He told me that he hadn't been happy at school, and that he'd been bullied. At first, I thought there was no way I could employ him. But as I continued to talk to him, I found myself warming to him. He hadn't been able to find employment, so he was working as a volunteer teacher's assistant at the school he'd recently left, just to get work experience. I liked that. I could see he was self-motivated and wanted to progress his life, and I believed that he would work hard. I decided to take a punt on him. It turned out to be one of the best decisions I ever made. Keith blossomed over the 13 years he was with us. He was a huge asset and ended up as the firm's head cashier – a position of enormous responsibility and trust – moving millions of pounds of clients' money every day. Eventually, Keith moved on to an even bigger position, and I will always be proud of helping get his career going.

Unfortunately, out of the tens of people we hired over the first few years of trading, Keith was a rare success. Many people came and went – sometimes their decision, sometimes ours. The cost of these recruitment mistakes was huge. Not only did we have to pay the salary of the new recruit, but often we'd also paid advertising costs and recruitment agency fees, not to mention the time spent on interviews, induction and training. And each time we realised we'd made a mistake, yet *more* time had to be spent on performance management and dealing with departure.

And the price wasn't just paid by us. The recruit would also pay dearly when it transpired they were not in the right job. They may have left a job they'd been happy in to come and work for us; they may even have relocated their family.

Perhaps most damaging of all were the client relationship costs. Clients didn't like it when our staff changed, and sometimes even preferred to move firms with the leaving member of staff.

I've always believed there are no bad people – just bad fits – so I felt a heavy burden of responsibility for these recruitment mistakes, and I became determined to work on making the process more successful.

7.2. A formal process

The first thing I did was to get some training myself, to learn best practice at the time. I then designed our recruitment procedure. This has evolved over the years (in fact, I don't think there's ever been a year when some change has not been made to it).

Now we require a clear decision to recruit approved at the highest level. A recruitment form must be completed, setting out the qualities of the person we need and specifying any change to our normal process. A written test must be set to assess skills. A named person must be responsible for the recruitment. We normally have two interviews – the first focusing on attitude and the second, which will usually include a partner, focusing on skills. Sometimes, for senior posts, there's a third interview – often over dinner.

No one is allowed to be responsible for a recruitment process unless they have taken our in-house training course.

7.3. EAGLES

Very early on, I noticed that we were often recruiting people like Annie who, although nice and good at her work, did not share our values.

I came up with a list of attributes and attitudes we were looking for in our new recruits – about 14 of them – things like *self-motivated, ambitious, wants to work in teams* – and we proudly called anyone who had these attributes a 'BB Professional'. Unfortunately, the list was so long that no one could remember it! We needed an easier way. Back to the drawing board I went, and I reduced the list to just six essentials. I wanted an acronym to make them memorable, and with a bit of reordering I came up with EAGLES.

EAGLES:

- want to <u>Exceed</u> client expectations. They care about clients and strive to improve clients' lives. They will go the extra mile when needed.

- are <u>Ambitious</u>, self-motivated, hungry. They thrive on exceeding targets.

- will put the <u>Greatest good</u> of the firm first – they are team players. They say 'we' not 'I' and will make personal sacrifices for the good of the firm.

- are <u>Learning</u> professionals. They want to be the best lawyer, the best receptionist, the best compliance manager – whatever they are, they want to be the best they can be.

- have the highest <u>Ethical</u> standards, the highest level of integrity. They will never compromise the client's best interests.

- are <u>Sociable</u> – they find work fun, and they want to join in and work with others. They have good personal relationships with other staff and with clients. People enjoy spending time with them. They pass the 'ski test' (would the interviewer like to spend a weekend skiing with them?)

Of course, EAGLES are what *we* are looking for, but this won't be the same for every organisation. What's important will depend on the values and culture of the organisation.

Now I had identified the kind of recruits we were looking for, I needed to make sure we found them. I redesigned our interview structure with questions designed to test each of the EAGLES criteria in turn. Now no candidate is able to go to second interview unless the first interviewer can confirm they're satisfied that all the EAGLES criteria are met.

7.4. Technical skills

I learnt early the importance of identifying the skills we need – we require these to be specified before any recruitment process can begin. It took longer to realise that even though a candidate had exam results or professional qualifications, it was a big mistake to take these skills as a given.

In the early days, we asked candidates to bring with them a piece of written work they were proud of; for example, a letter of advice to a client. We thought this would help us see the quality of their legal work and their writing style. Mostly this worked well, but on one occasion a candidate presented me with a letter that gave advice I didn't agree with, so I asked her a few questions about it at her interview. It soon transpired that it wasn't the candidate who'd drafted the advice at all, but her boss! After that, I made a point of always discussing written work with the applicant in some detail.

We've now refined this further and we always set a written test at our office, for every position. Our test is usually in two parts: a drafting exercise e.g. a letter to a fictitious client and some quick-fire questions to test factual knowledge. Sometimes we add a question that we don't expect an applicant to be able to answer – we want to know how they would tackle the problem. Law is our trade, and our clients need to be able to take it as a given that we are excellent lawyers. Regretfully, it does not always follow that if someone is a qualified solicitor, then they are a good lawyer. This test is not always popular with our senior people (who have to set and mark the test) or the potential recruits (some of whom have even refused to do it). But I've stood firm – there can be absolutely no excuse for recruiting someone without the necessary skills, and these are easily tested in a written exam and with some probing interview questions.

It is the job of the second interviewers to satisfy themselves that the applicant has the right technical skills. They will probe on the test results. They may set up a role play. They may talk about a current legal challenge we have for a client. Whatever it takes to be sure!

Of course, as I said before, the skills are not as important as the attitude but if there is a skill deficit such that training will be needed you need to be aware of this before making a job offer.

7.5. Common recruitment pitfalls

I spend a lot of time examining what has gone wrong when we make a recruitment mistake now. Each time I identify a problem, I make a tweak to our procedures or training. I believe there can be no better use of my time.

I've identified a number of common pitfalls in recruitment.

7.5.1. We just need a safe pair of hands!

One of the hardest things to resist is a 'safe pair of hands'. By that, I mean someone who is skilled in the work but who doesn't meet all of our EAGLES criteria. Recently a senior solicitor came to me late at night to discuss an interview. She was obviously shattered, and practically begging me. 'We have so much work – right now all I want is a safe pair of hands'. The pressure was enormous, and the choice was simple: find more staff, or turn client work away.

In the calm of a partners' meeting we'd made the decision to turn the work away rather than recruit a person who was not a good fit. But in practice, that's not so easy. Clients are precious, and we work hard to get more of them. Telling a client that we don't have the capacity to service their work is a difficult thing to do. Further, we reward our managers for growth, making it even harder for them to turn work away.

This pressure, of course, goes right to the top. A profit-sharing partner has a lot of good reasons to hire a lawyer who doesn't quite fit all our stringent EAGLES criteria. If we take on the work and do it profitably, then their profit share will be bigger. It's easy to take this short-term view when faced with a decision about an individual applicant and to forget what we agreed at the partners' meeting when we were talking about our long-term best interests.

7.5.2. They were the best applicant!

I used to hear this a lot. Somewhere along the way, the idea had slipped into our folklore that recruitment was simply a matter of advertising the position and picking the best of the bunch. This is a big mistake. If you recruit someone who does not share your values they will never be truly happy in your organisation. If you recruit someone without the necessary skills you will be faced with an unexpected choice – to invest in training them or to dismiss them.

Recruitment is not about picking the best of the bunch but continuing the search until you find someone who fulfils your criteria no matter how long it takes.

Lynne's I

7.5.3. We misled the applicant

Sometimes we recruit good people who leave shortl
with us. The reason is very often that we did not tell
of the truth about us and about our job.

Sometimes it's a culture thing. On arriving at work, they discover
that they don't share our values – maybe they don't agree that
delighting clients is more important than leaving the office
on time, or perhaps they don't like our very flexible working
environment and feel they need more boundaries or supervision.
Or it could be that they're disappointed with the quality of the
work – it's tempting at interview to 'big up' the quality of the
work on offer to attract a good applicant. What we must do at
interview is tell applicants the whole truth about us, warts and
all, so they can make their own judgement about whether we are
a good fit for them. One easy way is to make sure our values and
culture shine through on our websites – no one these days will
apply for a job without looking at the website. If our values are
not attractive to them, hopefully they won't waste their time and
ours by applying.

7.5.4. They were better than that at interview!

I hear this sometimes. It's important to remember that at interview,
we see applicants at their very best. The interview is usually not
very long, and it's quite easy for an applicant to put on a good
show and tell us what we want to hear. We now have written tests
and longer interviews to give more opportunity to get to know
applicants, but the lesson to learn is that if there's any problem
that is apparent at interview then it's likely to be magnified once
they become comfortable in the job!

I made a mistake when I hired a commercial lawyer who was just a
tiny bit dishevelled at his interview – his shirt was not quite white

and his cuffs were just a bit worn and he arrived without a pen. I overlooked it and that turned out to be a mistake. Although he was a competent lawyer it became clear that he was always just a bit scruffy and frequently disorganised. We found our solicitors were reluctant to refer their clients to him. Eventually he had to go.

7.5.5. We gave them a halo

It was a few years in before I noticed the 'halo effect'. Sometimes a colleague would return from an interview gushing with enthusiasm about an applicant. We would jump in and hire that person, excited to see what they could bring to the firm, and only then find problems that had been overlooked at interview.

As so often happens, I only recognised it when it happened to me. I engaged a solicitor who was from the north east of England, and who had a maths degree, which isn't all that common for a solicitor. Coming from a similar background, I immediately warmed to him and knew we'd enjoy working together. It was only after he started work when questions were raised about his legal ability that I noticed that I had I played down the fact he had a fairly average academic record, and skirted over some gaps in his CV. I realised that because I thought he was like me in background, I had assumed he'd be like me in work ability and ethic, too. I won't make that mistake again.

This is human nature – we like people like us. But recruitment isn't just about liking people. They need the right attitude and skills, too.

7.5.6. We made the wrong choice because we were scared

It was much more recently that I noticed another factor at play in recruitment. Sometimes we had more than one good candidate, and I began to notice a tendency to select the more junior one. Why would our recruiters frequently choose the *less experienced* candidate? It just didn't make sense. We had work at a level that justified the more senior candidate.

I think it is a fear of being outshone by a candidate you recruit to work for you – someone who turns out to be better than you. The reality is that this happens all the time – and it's a good thing for the firm! Remember, the recruitment bar must go up – we *must* hire people better than us.

As I look around at the top team in our firm, I see several partners who have leapfrogged over the person who recruited them! This can sometimes be a bitter pill. Sweeten it by recognising the great recruitment success. We all benefit from making the firm better, so take pride in good recruitment. In partners' meetings we sometimes joke that none of us would have been hired if we were applying to our firm today – and we congratulate ourselves on that!

This is one reason why it's really important that the most senior partners are involved in recruitment. They're more likely to be able to recognise the need to recruit the best – and, at the same time, to be able to reassure our existing staff that good people are not a threat but rather a way of making our firm better for all of us.

For the most senior level recruits, we always have at least two partners involved – we can then reassure each other!

7.6. Rigour and time

It's no good designing great systems if they're not followed. You have to follow the agreed process with rigour and ample allocation of time.

The HR team need to be the 'rigour police'. They can't be held responsible for recruitment decisions, but they can be accountable for making sure the process is followed. Importantly, they must be supported completely by the managing partner in this. It's often very senior people who think the process does not apply to them – that they can still go about recruitment in the way they always have – that must not be tolerated. The managing partner must endorse the fact that the process is not optional and that time spent on recruitment is time well spent at every level of the organisation.

Recruitment needs time – lots of it. It may take months to find the right applicant, and when you do, they're likely to have a long notice period. Time scales for filling a senior-level job vacancy are months, not weeks. It also takes time allocation from many people in the organisation – time to get clear on who exactly you're looking for, time to draft great advertisements that will tempt good people to apply, time to prepare tests and consider interview questions, and time to interview, which will be the time of your very best people. I don't think there's any more valuable use of your very best and most senior lawyers' time than in recruitment.

It's very frustrating when we have work but can't find people to do it. It's equally frustrating when we know that growth is constrained by not being able to find the right people to recruit. I love to see our firm grow and I find this so frustrating, but I know it's right. We are who we recruit, and every recruit makes the firm either a little better or a little worse. It's better to be smaller with great people! This is the way to business success.

7.7. Induction

When you have taken so much time to get the right people on board make sure you give them the very best chance of success with a comprehensive induction process. This is very important – good people want to get up and running as quickly as possible.

We dedicate the first two weeks of employment to learning our systems and lawyers have no chargeable time target during this period. Every new member of staff is allocated a 'buddy' to make sure they have someone in a similar role to befriend and ask the tricky first day questions of – where are the loos and how do I get the printer to work?

We work to a three-month induction plan including a meeting with the managing partner for core ideology, vision and values as well as the usual IT, compliance and HR training. An early formal meeting with the line manager will make sure expectations for the role are explicitly agreed.

Our induction period ends with a first appraisal – where, if all is well, the end of probation is confirmed and the first set of goals and a training plan are agreed.

7.8. It's working!

It is impossible to quantify the amount of time that's gone into trying to improve our recruitment process, and I hope we will never cease. And I'm pleased to report that it's working! We are now making fewer mistakes. I can see evidence of recruiters not settling for second-best, even when that means positions are vacant for a long time. I see more and more people around the place who really buy into our culture. I see happier teams, and I see better financial results. It's a wonderful, victorious spiral in action – good staff attract good clients who enable us to attract great staff who do great work and attract even better clients... And the excellent work goes on.

A few great questions

1. Have you taken the time to identify the personal attributes necessary for a new recruit to be happy in your firm? A good way of addressing this is to think about the attributes or values of your very best people.

2. When recruiting, are you specific about the skills that are needed? Are you clear whether you really need these from day one, or are you willing to train the right person? How are you going to test for the necessary skills for the role?

3. Who are the right people to make the decision for each position? Do they have the courage and determination to make only the right recruit – to select the very best? Are they ready to devote the time to it?

4. Do you have a rigorous recruitment system? Who is responsible for making sure it is followed?

5. Are all those who are involved in recruitment given full training in the process and in interview techniques?

Rule 8:
Free up their future!

Having looked at recruitment in the last Rule we now need to consider how to deal with the flip side of the coin; letting people go.

It's not fair to keep people in jobs where they are unhappy or consistently underperforming. Not fair on all the good people in the organisation who have to work harder to compensate for that person's underperformance, and not fair on the poorly performing person either. It is best for everyone to take the decision, after fair process, to 'free up their future'.

We only want to work with happy people, and we want everyone to be happy at work. My own test is this – I want to go to work looking forward to my day at least nine out of every ten days, and I want that for all those who work with me too. I also want to be able to say that everyone I work with, on nine out of every ten days has made a positive contribution to the firm – and if I can't say that then I think it is time their futures were freed up!

Of course, first we would try and resolve any problems – if the issues can be resolved that is better for everyone. How long we give that and how much effort we expend will depend on individual circumstances. A fair approach is very important – and it should go without saying that, where appropriate, we must comply with the law as well as our own procedures.

8.1. Make a decision

Sometimes the decision to dismiss someone comes easily – when a red line has been crossed and the person has to go. I never struggled to dismiss people who were dishonest or who did not seem to care about their work or our clients. Of course, we must still follow proper process – but I don't lose sleep at night when decisions are made for these reasons.

Other times, however, it can be very difficult.

Our first casualty after we started Bolt Burdon was Annie, our word processor operator who didn't understand urgency. We all liked Annie and she was good at her job but she did not understand, or maybe she didn't care, that if she could not produce documents swiftly there were consequences for our clients. Eventually, after nearly a year of her employment with us, it was crunch time. We decided she had to go. It was hard because we liked her so much. Roger and I decided we must do the deed together, and we called her into my office. We carefully and very apologetically broke the news to Annie that her employment was terminated, and held our breath. But she wasn't upset, as we'd feared. Instead, she lit up like a Christmas tree. 'Oh, thank you so much,' she said. 'I really want to go and sing in a band, but I like you all here and I didn't want to let you down. You've helped make my decision for me!' We were all delighted – we truly had freed up Annie's future!

It doesn't always have such a happy ending.

8.2. Name the problem

It isn't always easy to identify the people who are pulling the business down. Over the years I've come across a few problems that, once named, have been easier to spot.

8.2.1. Just not a great lawyer

Trevor was a nice guy. He fitted in well, he worked hard to try to please his clients, and he was well liked in the firm. What it took us years to work out, however, was that he was just not a great lawyer. It wasn't until I became his manager that I noticed that he was never bringing legal issues to me to discuss. When I asked him about his cases I noticed he often told me what the barrister had to say – but rarely offered his own view of the law. I never discovered if it was a lack of brainpower or a lack of passion but, either way, once we'd put our finger on the problem, it was clear he had to go.

8.2.2. Loves the law – clients not so much!

Jack was completely different. Jack was exceptionally clever and a very good lawyer. He really cared about the law and enjoyed interesting legal arguments – sometimes to the point of annoyance! But I respected that. I also enjoy interesting debates about how far you can push the legal concept of 'coming to equity with clean hands' or the debateable duty of care to people who are not clients. Jack was promoted several times – I desperately wanted him to succeed in our firm – building a firm of good lawyers was so important to me. But eventually I had to face the truth. Jack might be an outstanding lawyer, but delighting clients was not important to him. I was getting too many phone calls from clients who were complaining about delay, and nagging Jack to get work done was exhausting me!

8.2.3. The 'it's all about the fees' lawyer

There are some lawyers who forget that the work they do has to be proportionate to the problem. They are so involved in researching the law, finding the best solution, racking up chargeable hours, doing what lawyers do that they forget there is a client who wants a practical, value for money, result.

Giving practical legal advice has always been important to us – and advice where the result is just not worth the cost is not good advice for the client. These lawyers often do great work then send their clients huge bills and then wonder why the client complains!

8.2.4. The admin avoider

I know. It's not fun (like debates about the law) or joyous (like hearing 'Wow, *thank you!*' from a client). Some might even say it's boring. But good administration is an essential part of any successful business.

For us time recording is a non-negotiable task. Stuart was still in his probation period, and simply would not do his time recording. He didn't see the value in it and was very happy to chat endlessly about his reasons for not doing it. After several stern words with him, I issued a 'work instruction' that he must record his time every evening before he left the office. Still it did not get done. Finally, I'd had enough, and decided that as nice as he was, he could not work here, and held a termination meeting. Stuart was very surprised and upset when he realised what was happening. He liked working for us! He begged me to give him a second chance. I gave in and agreed – one more chance. Two weeks later, we were back in the same room because he hadn't done his time recording. This time, though, I did indeed succeed in terminating his contract. A lesson learnt. I am sure Stuart will be successful at something – I really liked him. I hope he has found a job with less admin where he is enjoying his 'freed up' future!

8.2.5. The muddler

Alison's philosophy in life was to 'muddle through'. She was incredibly willing and would turn her hand to anything, but always preferred to do it her way. We have strong systems, but Alison often thought she had an easier way. Maybe she did, I would have welcomed her suggestions had she offered them, but she just muddled through, getting things done in her own 'easier' way.

It was only after she'd left that we learnt the true extent of the damage. Alison was responsible for indexing our title deeds before putting them in the safe. After she left, we couldn't find some of the deeds in our system. Eventually we discovered many deeds that hadn't been properly indexed. Alison had indeed found an 'easier' way, just putting the physical deeds in store, without indexing at all! It took weeks to check all our deeds and make sure they were properly scanned and indexed. Thankfully all the missing deeds were located but not without the cost of paying someone to repeat all the work that Alison should have done.

Muddlers are incredibly dangerous. Their whole outlook is short-term. Their attitude is to make every job as easy as possible for today, or to do whatever it takes just to get the boss off their back. If a muddler comes across a problem in the organisation, they'll either sweep it under the carpet or stick a plaster on it. They will not look for the underlying system problem and invest time in getting that resolved.

8.2.6. The bully

Bullies are very hard to spot – they generally know they're a bully and go to great lengths to hide the fact. In my 30 years of management, we've had two bullies in our firm (that I know about). Derek was our first. He'd worked for us for several years before I dismissed him for a reason that had nothing to do with bullying. After he'd gone, I found out that he'd actually threatened junior staff with 'I will tell Lynne'. He'd created a team who were terrified of making a mistake or a suggestion, and who were terrified of me! We had several very unhappy staff members, and most upsetting of all for me was how long this had gone on before it came to my attention.

After Derek went, I changed my managing partner's speech at the induction meeting with new staff. At that meeting we now tell staff that if 'really bad stuff' is happening to them – bullying, discrimination, harassment – they are to tell the managing partner immediately, who will agree with them the best way to address the problem.

This was a step in the right direction, but it was clearly not enough. We had a second bully, who worked for us for several years before anyone found the courage to tell me about it. It was swiftly resolved but I still feel very sad about this. We continue to work really hard to make sure our working environment is healthy and that any unpleasant people are ousted.

8.2.7. The gentle underminer

Tandy was a secretary and she was an 'underminer'. On the face of it, Tandy walked the talk, she was very skilled at her job and she commanded fierce loyalty and support from her immediate boss.

But Tandy loved to stir and gossip. At every opportunity, by the kettle or in the pub, she would – with a carefully selected audience – have a moan. Her sentences would start with 'Did you know, they're talking about…'. She'd exaggerate every story. If someone left, she'd always put a spin on it that was damaging to the organisation. If someone she didn't like was promoted she might suggest that we had made a mistake in promoting them and that they were not up to the new job.

Underminers often last so long because they're very good at their job. They're quick to earn a halo from their managers, who will often fight for them and protect them. But they're not worth it! Underminers may not even realise what damage they are causing but they can do untold harm to the organisation in a hundred tiny little ways…

8.2.8. The bad apple

Bad apples are even worse than underminers. They may or may not be good at their job but they have become discontented and seek to cause damage to the organisation. They proactively spread discontent – trying to infect the whole barrel! They work to build support for their cause, gathering a group of people who bond tightly together over whatever it is they perceive as unsatisfactory or unjust.

Bad apples can be incredibly damaging. People love to belong to groups – you need to work very hard to ensure that all bonding is around the firm's values and culture and not around the bad apple's moans.

8.2.9. The reluctant litigator

You read that right! I've come across this a few times now – the litigator who hates litigating! We've always had a big litigation practice. Our philosophy has always been to issue proceedings early and get the court timetable underway to add pressure to the negotiations. This is nearly always in the clients' best interests.

The reluctant litigator is easy to spot when you know how. First, they will delay issuing proceedings as long as possible. When proceedings are actually issued – which they have to be within strict time limits – the reluctant litigator will ask the court for stays (a temporary halt to the court timetable), time extensions (an agreed longer time frame for the next step)... anything but actually getting before a judge and asking the court to decide!

Barbara was the world expert in litigation reluctance. She acted for the families of babies who were brain-damaged at birth due to medical negligence. Her clients loved her. It took us three years to realise that while she had been with us she hadn't concluded a single case! The work was good, but she would do almost anything to avoid pushing the case to conclusion in the courts.

8.2.10. The problem-toter

I was chatting to a colleague and I mentioned in passing that Fred had discussed an interesting question with me. My colleague said he had discussed it with him too. On further enquiry, I found four more people with whom Fred had discussed the same issue!

This came down to a basic lack of confidence, an inability to decide on a course of action for himself, so Fred would effectively run opinion polls on what to do. This approach takes too much time from too many people, racking up a cost to the firm that's out of all proportion to the decision to be made. The lack of confidence needs to be addressed – clear guidance needs to be given about which one person to discuss problems with. But ultimately, if after sufficient support, a solicitor is unable to make decisions you have to conclude they are not up to the job.

8.2.11. What about the 'parked ones'?

A dilemma we've often been faced with is when to bend our own rules. We aim to recruit only people who are ambitious – those who are hungry and want to rise through our organisation. But what to do with the employee who is pleasing the clients, doing good, solid work, but is not ambitious and never quite meets the criteria for promotion? We say they are 'parked'; still a good car but going nowhere!

This is one area where we have been able to compromise. We've decided there is space in our organisation for those who do share our values and who do good work but who do not seek more responsibility, who don't want to move up – who wish to remain 'parked'.

Where we have made a mistake, though, is in promoting such people. This has usually happened when there was a bit of a feeling of embarrassment all round – '*been here five years and still no promotion...*' It is a mistake to promote them. They go from performing well in a job they're happy with to underperforming in a job they never really wanted to do.

8.3. The price of doing nothing

The cost of having the wrong people in the organisation is huge.

Client relationships may be damaged, either because the person is not a good lawyer or has not provided good service (in which case after their departure we may struggle to rebuild the client relationship) or, worse, because they *are* a good lawyer, and the client likes them, but they're damaging the business in another way (in which case, when they eventually leave, there's a risk that the client will want to follow them).

Our reputation is also very likely to be damaged, either because of unhappy clients or because, when we do eventually find the courage to dismiss, the person leaves with resentment and bad-mouths the firm to as many people as they can get to listen.

There is, however, an even bigger risk of keeping underperformers – the risk of losing good staff. The right people want to work with like-minded people – other EAGLES. They do not want to work in a firm that tolerates underperformers. If we allow people to stay who do not share our core values, the EAGLES will start to fly away.

And yet, even this is not the biggest risk of all.

If you have too many underperformers in the organisation, it becomes the 'organisational norm'. Every time we accept a level of underperformance for one person, we're saying to all the others, 'Never mind what we said when we set your goals at your appraisal, we didn't really mean that. This lower level is fine.' And this is a very difficult situation to get out of. It needs courage and determination – and maybe even an acceptance that there will be a short-term financial cost. It was about ten years ago that we realised we'd made this very mistake. We were at a partners' retreat in the Hertfordshire countryside when we realised that we'd taken our eye off the ball and amassed quite a few people in our organisation who didn't make the grade. We divided all our staff into three lists: 'keepers', 'not yet sure' and 'must go'. Before long, we had about ten people on the 'must go' list. That was not a happy day.

When we returned to the office the next day, we commenced proper performance management for all our underperformers.

Within a year, all those on the 'must go' list had all gone – not one of them had been ready or able to make the changes we needed.

I've spent a huge amount of time reflecting on it, but it always comes back to this: remember, every day you keep an underperforming person without taking any action is a day you vote for the firm not being the best it can be.

8.4. Inbuilt checks

The organisation needs to have check points where the question is asked: Is this person an asset to our organisation?

The first check will be at the end of the probation period – at this time employment will be confirmed, the probation period extended or the employment terminated. We do this at between three to six months. This is also when we do a first appraisal when goals are set and training plans developed. This is the time to identify any early problems and put in place plans to rectify them.

Line managers will meet with their staff at least monthly. Problems should be addressed early – initially informally and if that doesn't work, formally in our performance procedure. It's important to get the process going as soon as problems are identified so that if improvement is needed the new staff member can be given time to sort things out.

We always have a 'last-chance check' when a new recruit has been with us for 18 months. This is a discussion between the managing partner and the line manager, and is the last chance to identify any issues and address them – and then if they are not resolved dismiss within the two-year limit without any risk of unfair dismissal.

It's necessary to have rigorous processes to ensure that if recruitment mistakes are made, the employee knows what's going wrong from the earliest possible moment and has every chance to improve. For those who can't make the grade an early exit is in everyone's best interests.

Sometimes problems arise with a person who has worked with us for a long time. These problems are often more difficult to spot – we tend to assume people will behave as they always have. When a new problem is identified the first thing should always be an honest conversation. Find out what's going on. Are there personal issues we need to be aware of? Maybe the job has just got boring and the employee has grown and needs a change – a good person may just need a new stimulus. I was a commercial property lawyer for many years – I enjoyed that work but I was beginning to feel stale. I was completely reenergised when I was able to change my career to full time managing partner – not everyone has that luxury. If someone's no longer a good fit, or if they're underperforming, they're unlikely to be happy. Step one is always to get to the root of the problem.

For those who have been loyal but have now become stale, you and they deserve whatever is needed to help them to happiness. Sometimes unhappy people just need a little help to make the decision for themselves. They may not realise it's time to make new decisions about their life plan and move on. In the 1990s we started sending four people each year to the John Ridgeway School of Adventure[14] at Ardmore in the far north-west of Scotland. Roger and I had both done this course and loved it! It was not a holiday – we both thought at times we were about to die! It was a week-long, outward-bound-type course for business people. After a couple of years of sending people there, we noticed that many were returning having had an amazing experience – then resigning. We discussed for a while – should we stop sending them? No, on the contrary – they were going, and growing, and realising that we were not the right firm for them. That was money well spent.

8.5. So what holds us back?

The arguments for freeing up the future of underperforming staff are overwhelming – so why don't we do it? I've often asked myself why we're so bad at this. What is it that stops us from taking action sooner?

8.5.1. Shared fault

The first reason may be guilt. Perhaps guilt at the recruitment mistake? Perhaps guilt for not recognising a problem earlier – or maybe we spotted it and failed to act? Maybe the person was a good performer in the past, but something has now changed – is that our fault? Support for the manager having to make the difficult decision is important here. If they have made a mistake and failed to deal with a problem promptly, reminding them that they also have a duty to the others in their team and the firm will help them feel better about tackling the problem now.

8.5.2. Competing values

We have values about the sort of people we want to employ – EAGLES – but we also value treating people fairly and with respect. We sometimes have to talk about dismissing people we really like and with whom we've had some great times. We don't want to hurt their feelings or damage their careers.

This is where the values hierarchy has to be clear – all these values are valid and important but ultimately one has to come above the other. For us, the most important value is always 'firm first'. We have to do what's right by our clients and our good people.

If someone is not measuring up, they have to go. The 'firm first' value – putting our clients and our firm first – makes it easier to accept that and to take the necessary action.

8.5.3. Wasting sunk costs

Another thing that holds us back and keeps us hanging on to wishful thinking is when we've invested a lot of time and energy in someone, it's very hard to draw the line and give up.

You have to forget the sunk costs. You're only throwing good money after bad! The biggest cost of all is keeping going. Remember: every day you keep an underperformer, you're voting for clients to get less than you want to give them, for damage to your reputation and for profits to be less than they could be.

8.5.4. Staff turnover statistics

People get very worried about staff turnover figures. These are often reported in the legal press. I'm a huge believer in 'what you measure is what you get'. If you're worried about measuring turnover, it's likely you'll hang onto bad fits far too long. I believe there are more important things to measure, e.g. what is the turnover of 'good' people – the people we would have preferred to stay or, how quickly are the 'bad fits' departing – the sooner the better?

The point is this – a bad fit is one of two things:

- A recruitment mistake. If this is the case, the sooner you realise it, the better. But this is not a turnover problem, this is a recruitment problem.

- Someone who was a 'good fit' and now is not. If that person was once someone you wanted to be on the bus with, you need to work out what's changed and sort it out.

A 'turnover problem' is when you have too many 'good fits' leaving – people that you would have preferred to stay. That is when you are failing to keep your good people happy. I address what you can do about this in Rules 9, 10 and 11.

8.5.5. Communication of the departure

'But everybody likes them! The fallout will be terrible!' This may be true, but it's back to that values conflict. When you're clear about the reason for making a decision, when you're completely confident that you're doing right by your values, then the decision to terminate is easy.

But telling the rest of the firm is undeniably difficult. As a manager, you might be celebrating the resignation – an underperformer has gone! Yet you can't explain that to the whole firm – that would be disrespectful to the departing person. On the other hand, people can be very unsettled by unexplained departures, and that departing employee might be bad-mouthing their manager or the partners – and it's very unlikely they'll be telling even their friends the whole truth.

This is a very difficult line to tread. My belief is that it's best to say as much as possible whilst respecting the privacy and reputation of the person departing. This is really important, because people will know that how you respect the person leaving now is how you'll respect *them* if they decide to leave.

8.6. One last thing

It's always worth doing an exit interview. It's a real opportunity to learn something, even if it's something quite small. The best person to conduct it is someone just a little removed from the departing person – in our case normally the HR manager.

People who are departing on good terms will usually want to do the best by the firm if we've treated them well, and on departure are likely to be very willing to open up and say what they truly think.

People departing on bad terms may relish the opportunity to release their stream of venom! But it's still worth listening carefully. In the cold light of day, was there a grain of truth in the vitriol? Something you can change to make the firm that little bit better, and your people that little bit happier? And maybe you should ask yourself why you didn't know sooner how they felt!

8.7. Just imagine

Just imagine how great the firm would be if there were no 'bad fits' or underperformers. Imagine a firm where every single member of staff is committed to the business culture, where everyone's hitting all their performance measures and where everyone's happy in their work. That is a firm I would want to work for. That is a firm I would want to instruct to do my work. That is, indeed, success!

A few great questions

1. Are there any people in your organisation/team who have been with you for more than a year who you are still not sure are 'good fits'? How are you going to decide? Do you have robust procedures in place to make sure the two-year point will not pass unnoticed?

2. How many people have left your organisation/team during the last year who you've been sorry to lose? Do you know why they went? Are you sure? Do you have a problem that needs solving before you lose more good people for the same reason?

3. Try the three-column test. List every person in your organisation/team in one of three columns – a 'keeper', a 'not sure yet' or a 'must go'. Do you have a serious problem?

4. Do you do exit interviews, and review them in management meetings, to see what can be learnt?

RULE 9:
Don't mess up the basics!

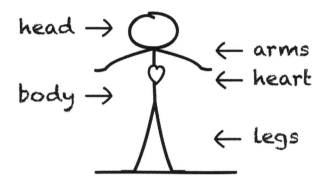

head →

body →

← arms
← heart

← legs

Finding the right people – and freeing up the future of the wrong ones – is not easy. When you do get good people you must work really hard to keep them.

The first step is to make sure that you do not make your people unhappy! Get the basics right and make sure that there is no cause for complaint and nothing for anyone to worry about.

We're wired to look for danger – things that might go wrong. People will notice the smallest things that suggest threat! If anything's not right, they will worry about it.

We are also wired to seek common causes to bond around – small things that make life more difficult than necessary, or which do not feel fair are perfect candidates for a bit of bonding!

So make sure that your people feel secure and have the basic things they need, so they can be free to focus on doing their best work. This is in everyone's best interests. Any failure on providing these basics creates things to moan about, bad chat around the kettle and gives ammunition to any bad apples to build support for their cause!

9.1. What are the basics?

9.1.1. Maslow's hierarchy

It was way back in 1943 that Abraham Maslow presented his now very well-known hierarchy of human needs.[15]

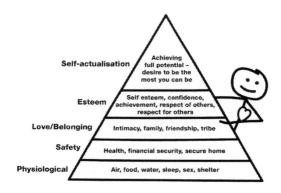

The most basic needs for us as humans are physiological: air, food, water, shelter, sex and sleep. Without these, we cannot survive.

When these needs are satisfied, we become concerned with safety: health, financial security and a secure home. When we feel safe we want social belonging – feelings of friendship, intimacy, family. If we have all of these, we become concerned with matters of esteem – we seek to be accepted and valued by others, and by ourselves. Only then can we move to self-actualisation – realising our full potential and self.

Work, for most of us, provides safety (financial security) and social belonging (to the organisation). For many of us it will also give us esteem and maybe one day even self-actualisation. But the 'basics' for work are safety and social belonging – without these we cannot do our best work.

9.1.2. How our brains work

With the neuroscience we know now, it's easy to understand why these needs of safety and belonging must come first.

The very oldest part of our brain (our reptilian brain) is concerned with keeping us physically safe. It's very fast and, if we feel under threat of physical harm, it will make decisions for us without any conscious thought. If you fear for your physical safety, you will fight or run or hide – you won't stop to think through the options first. This part of the brain will be active whenever we feel physically unsafe.

As we developed into mammals, a second part of our brain developed (our mammalian brain, which includes the amygdala – the part that constantly scans the environment for threat). Signals travel through our mammalian brain just a bit slower than through our reptilian brain. The mammalian brain is concerned with being accepted, keeping us safe from judgement and helping us conform so we remain welcome in our tribe. It's this part of the brain that tries to stop us doing unconventional things – it worries about what other people think. This part of the brain will be active whenever we feel we do not belong or are being judged.

Our human brain (the neocortex – and more specifically the prefrontal cortex) is newer and much slower than the other parts of the brain. It's where we do our logical and creative thinking – where we do our best work. This is the brain we want to be using at work. The problem is that as soon as we perceive any threat, our reptilian or mammalian brain takes over and the human brain is taken offline until our animals are happy again!

If we're worried about something, or overwhelmed with the quantity of work we have to do, these are threats. The ancient parts of our brain will try to protect us, and we may find ourselves reverting to unhelpful behaviours – being grumpy or snappy (fight), watching endless TV or eating and drinking excessively (flight) or agreeing to something and then not doing it (freeze).

A few years ago, I was chatting to my daughter as we walked on the beach about a coaching question I'd been exploring. The question was 'Who am I really?' Without much hesitation, she replied, 'You're two different people. *Work-Lynne* is stressed, practical, regimented, analytical, strict, stern and serious. And *Lynne-Lynne* is chilled, funny, lively, approachable, loving. Guess which one I prefer to be around!'

Ouch! It seems that at work I have often been stressed and living in my animal brains! I feel sure my colleagues would also prefer *Lynne-Lynne* to arrive at the office each day!

9.1.3. Herzberg's Hygiene and Motivational Factors

In the early 1960s, Frederick Herzberg[16] proposed his 'two factor theory', that in the workplace there is one set of factors that causes job satisfaction (satisfiers) and a second set that causes dissatisfaction (dissatisfiers).

The dissatisfiers include basic working conditions, job security, salary, holiday, administrative procedures and relationships with colleagues, and they just need to be 'good enough'. Improving them beyond 'good enough' will not lead to greater motivation. These are the 'basics' of this Rule – the things necessary in the workplace for Maslow's lower order needs to be met.

The satisfiers include challenging work, recognition for achievement, responsibility, advancement, meaningful work, involvement in decision making. These things are to do with Maslow's higher order needs and I discuss these in Rule 10.

9.2. How to provide them

The basics for people to do their best work are that they need to feel safe and to have a sense of belonging. They need to feel the basics of their employment are fair.

9.2.1. Trust

It's essential that your employees trust you to live the stated values of the organisation, trust you to do the right thing, trust you to provide a fair and safe work environment and to offer support when it is needed, and trust you to keep promises. I don't think any employee can feel safe otherwise.

Trust has to be earned. It builds over hours, days, weeks and years, as your staff get to know you and feel able to understand and predict how you will behave.

Trust can be shattered in an instant. One lie found out, one promise not delivered, and trust goes out the window – and it's very, very difficult to rebuild.

9.2.2. Financial safety

As Maslow points out, we need to know we can keep the roof over our heads and the food on our table. Your employees need to know that their salary will be paid at the end of each month without having to worry about it. For this, it's important that people believe in the organisation's financial stability.

Your employees need to understand the way a business works at its simplest level – we (the partners) employ staff and pay their salaries and other business expenses – we do work for clients – we send invoices for the work done – the clients pay their bills. We must finance the gap between paying salaries so that the work can be done and getting paid by the clients. Managing this gap is the essence of managing cash flow.

Managing the cash flow without causing worry is a tricky business as it's very easy to give the wrong message. What people are likely to hear on a daily basis are phrases like, 'Do you have money on account from the client for that disbursement?' 'Have you chased that unpaid bill?' and 'That's too much to spend on the Christmas party!' Leaders need to take time to explain why these issues are being raised. It's not because we're about to go bust; it's simply good business management, and good cash flow enables us to invest more in the business and its people.

A few years ago, I was talking to a solicitor about the need to pay a large amount on behalf of a client, and that it was essential that the client pay us the money before we spend it. I was asked 'Why don't we just pay it out of the office account?' When I asked the solicitor what they thought the 'office account' was, he had no idea. He was very surprised when I explained it was really just a partners' joint bank account used for office expenses – if the account was overdrawn, then it was our personal liability; and if there was money in it, we could choose to use it to pay that client expense or to take our families on holiday! I think that in general, we're too secretive about business finances. This shouldn't be a taboo subject. It's good for everyone to understand the basics of how the business is financed. Of course, if there really are financial difficulties that need resolving, these must be the leaders' top priority. It would not be wise to talk about them too much, as it would jeopardise that feeling of financial safety.

9.2.3. Job security

Anyone who fears for the security of their job will be under threat. There are many reasons, other than the financial security of the firm, why a job may not be secure.

For example, you may make a strategic decision to stop doing a particular type of work, which will result in a whole team being made redundant. The best you can do here is make a swift decision and communicate it openly. At the same time, communicate your plans to help retrain staff or where that is not possible explain how you will help them find alternative employment. If this is an isolated decision, make this very clear, and give the reasons why you've decided to terminate just this one area of work. State that there are no plans to close any other part of the firm – because if that's left unsaid, people will be left wondering!

Sometimes an individual's job is under threat because of their own underperformance. Again, all you can do is be honest and fair. Remember, it's in the best interests of everyone to manage this swiftly and fairly – for the benefit of the underperforming person and also those who work with them.

9.2.4. Health

I've never had poor health, but I do fear it. I can't imagine how scary it must be to be so unwell you can't work and have to depend on benefits. I know that many people cope with work and serious health issues, often quietly and without fuss. Sometimes these issues are visible; sometimes not.

I believe that all of us have some part of our body that doesn't quite function as well as normal and that we learn to cope with this on a day-to-day basis. I can't spell and I have trouble getting dates right – hard as I try I just can't see my errors. I used to cope by carrying a tiny dictionary and diary in my handbag – until my phone replaced them both! The point is I think we all have to identify and make adaptations for our own personal health issues.

At work we need to create an environment where people can be helped to manage their own health as best they can, so that they can be free of health worry and able to do their best work.

We need to make sure the premises are safe, that people have eye tests and workstation assessments if they need them. But in a law firm, by far the biggest health risk is stress.

When we feel threatened, adrenalin and cortisol are released in our brains – this brings our animal brains online. It makes us feel vulnerable and alone. The problem is that with work stress, unlike with a physical threat, it's rarely over in an instant and it can go on for days, weeks or months: the immense pressure of a client deadline, a looming trial, a difficult client who makes you feel inadequate, or a mistake you have made where there may be a negligence claim against you. It is often one stress after another so the cortisol never gets a chance to properly dissipate.

There are now an ever increasing number of studies that show this ever present cortisol can make us severely ill.[17] There is also increasing evidence that a strong, supportive organisational culture makes all the difference.[18] When we feel trust and loyalty, serotonin and oxytocin are released, making us feel good. The presence of these chemicals reduces cortisol. In other words, if you create a friendly, supportive organisation, your staff will be healthier.

Make sure your people are aware of the risks they face in their job and do all you can to help them minimise them. You can offer training on how to recognise stress (we all have our own predictable behaviours – my own are getting grumpy, snappy, rushing around, unable to make simple decisions, eating standing up and eventually screaming or crying) and how to be more resilient (the key is not to get tougher, but to get proper recovery[19]). You can encourage everyone to take proper breaks and real holidays – without their emails! You can encourage healthy bodies and minds by providing exercise classes, gym memberships, yoga or meditation. And you should also make sure your managers are trained to watch for signs of stress or overwhelm – and know who to talk to for help in managing this.

Most important is to make sure each person accepts their health as their own responsibility but also feels able to ask you for help early if needed.

9.2.5. Belonging

Maslow identifies the need for love and belonging. Our mammalian brains are wired to help us stay included in the tribe – to make sure we conform to accepted behaviours. When we feel we belong, serotonin and oxytocin are released in our brains. We enjoy pulling together and working as a team. Our human brain is online and we're able to do our best work.

These days, most of us spend more of our lives at work than we do at home, so it's incredibly important that we feel we 'belong' at work. Fortunately, this feeling is easy to create. We can encourage that sense of belonging by getting our organisational structure right and by planning many integrating mechanisms to make sure people feel connected.

Structure – tribes and families

In the 1990s, Robin Dunbar[20] suggested that our brain size limits us to maintaining social relationships with about 150 people. I used to pride myself on knowing the name of everyone in our organisation, and just a little bit about them – enough to be able to have a chat around the kettle. But I realised that when we got to around 120 people, this was no longer possible. I suppose those last 30 spaces were reserved for the others in my life!

I've certainly observed 'growing pains' in the firm. When we started in 1986, there were five of us. We were all friends, and it was great. Roger went shopping on Wednesdays and then cooked us all lunch! There was a real family feel. In 1988, when we'd grown to ten people, lunch became bought-in sandwiches. By 1991, there were 16 of us, and we had to give up the firm lunch. The group became so big that many were afraid to speak, and fun had turned into a chore. This was about the time that we brought in Harry – the consultant who'd found that staff morale was low.

A troubled time followed while we tried to sort out our management structure. Things began to improve when I began to take it seriously! I was helped by the property recession of the early 1990s – I suddenly found I had a lot of time available for management training.

We never looked back.

We developed our team structure – family-sized groups, each built around a common area of work or clients, and with common goals or targets. Team members share work within the team according to skills and experience. By 1994, when we were 45 people, another staff survey was done for our Investors in People assessment – we waited nervously for the feedback but we need not have worried – our efforts had paid off and we were thrilled: staff morale was very high!

When I decided to split the firm in 2003, there were just fewer than 150 of us – that number again. Maybe we'd had a stroke of luck and got in there just before any trouble that might have been caused when we exceeded that size. Or maybe our size was a factor in bringing about the split, unknown to us at the time. Either way, it worked well for us. I've become a great believer in the 'team' – a group that's small enough for everyone to know each other well, and where no one is afraid to speak.

But how big is a team? My own experience is that smaller is better – a size where the whole team can go out to dinner and talk around one table. For us, one leader with about four or five others makes a great team. I have observed that when the dinner table gets to eight people there are often two conversations. Teams of less than eight give enough range of expertise, while still holding onto that feeling of all working together as one team towards a common goal. It allows everyone to feel heard. It creates a strong sense of belonging.

Integrating mechanisms

For the organisation to remain cohesive, it's really important that everyone feels they belong to the whole organisation – not just their own work team. If they don't, then silos will develop – which may ultimately put the organisation at risk of division.

I believe it's really important to make sure people form bonds across teams. There can be no downside. The upside is a more cohesive organisation where information gets shared for the benefit of the clients and everyone. The holy grail is that people feel they belong to the firm first and the team second.

There are hundreds of ways you can encourage friendships, and thus idea sharing, across teams: shared eating and relaxing spaces; lots of firm-wide celebrations, like impromptu drinks after a big success; shared challenges, like a marathon; shared fitness classes; clubs for bridge, theatre etc. The list is endless.

If you think these things sound like unnecessary frills, you are, in my view, very mistaken. They are absolutely essential in creating that firm-wide sense of belonging.

9.2.6. Salary and benefits

Everyone wants to feel they're being paid fairly. There are two things that will cause discontent – a perception that pay is not fair compared with market rates, or a perception that pay is not fair compared with colleagues.

It's relatively easy these days to find out the market rate for any position. The most reliable way is to see what new applicants are expecting, and what they're being paid in their current position. Don't forget to take into account any other benefits – pension contributions, health or life insurance, etc. My own view is that you should always aim to pay a bit above the market rate to minimise the risk of anyone feeling their pay is poor – but not too far above it. As Herzberg suggested, this will not give you any further benefit. Although getting it wrong will leave people dissatisfied, paying excessive salaries is not beneficial. The reason the salary got to the excessive level will be soon forgotten, and overpaying causes problems. For the employer, there's no going back if performance plummets. For the employee, if the salary can't be matched elsewhere, they may be tempted to stay in a job they're no longer happy in. Also, I think there are better ways to spend this money – read on to Rules 10 and 11!

Salaries within the organisation will be discussed between staff members – be in no doubt about this. This can be a problem if an individual feels they should be paid the same or more than a colleague. But you will be able to deal with any discontent as long as you're clear why two people, who on the face of it seem to be doing a similar job, are paid different amounts. I do believe salary should be paid on merit – not on years' experience – but this means you're likely to have to deal with questions as to why person X is paid more than person Y who may have more years under her belt. Make sure you know why and say so – even if you can't say specifically what someone else is earning you can clarify where their job or performance can be distinguished.

9.2.7. Working environment

Herzberg mentions working conditions, policies and administrative practices as potential demotivators. Some of this is obvious – people want to work for an organisation that supports them in the most basic way. An office building that is opened on time, a computer that works and is swiftly mended when it doesn't, a support team that does copying and scanning accurately and on time. These are basics and cause huge discontent if they're not right.

The physical working environment is also very important, but the problem here is that people don't all want the same thing! I like my desk and the space around it to be clean and free from junk. (That's how I like my home too – clean surfaces – minimal photos or ornaments!) As we know, others are the opposite – they want their own space, free to decorate that as they wish with family photos, tinsel and fairy lights, and ten pairs of shoes under the desk! I recently visited the Zappos headquarters in downtown Las Vegas. I've wanted to go there for years after reading Tony Hsieh's book *Delivering Happiness*.[21] I love so much about the Zappos culture, but on visiting the office I realised I could never work there – the physical environment was chaos! Desks decorated for birthdays, a dog crèche in the middle of the work floor, old creative installations that now seemed unloved and dusty around the place... not for me!

There is no easy solution to this. I guess at the end of the day you just have to make your decision and realise that about half the world will love it – and the other half will not. Oh, to have an office big enough for spaces to please everyone!

We need to recognise too that the office is not the only place people work. Clients' premises, on the train, at home – we must properly support healthy working in these places.

9.2.8. Policies and administrative procedures

Robust policies and operating procedures are essential for a well-run business. We live in a world where red tape is everywhere and compliance is a profession. Good administration is important to everyone, e.g. payroll administration must be perfect – no one wants to worry about being paid the wrong salary. However, what seems like unnecessary administration, e.g. a very complicated procedure to reclaim small amounts of petty expenditure, will cause discontent.

My philosophy is as few rules as possible – but when you do have a rule or procedure know why it exists and insist on it being observed by everyone.

9.2.9. Support in other areas of life

People don't just work. They have a life outside of the office too. If someone has personal problems at home, they won't be able to focus on doing their best work. It's hard to get this right. As an employer you can't be intrusive, but you do want to be kind. So often a tiny gesture – some friendly advice, maybe a salary advance or paying for a medical consultation – can help a distressed employee.

Many years ago, a member of staff was chatting to me in the kitchen. She was distressed because her mother's boiler had broken in her council house. The council were not responding, and she didn't have the money to fix it. The cost wasn't much, so we offered to pay for the boiler to be fixed. For us this was nothing, but I have never, ever received such overwhelming thanks – clearly a huge weight was lifted. I tell this story because it's really important that as our incomes increase we remain connected to the day-to-day realities of our staff members who may be struggling financially. No one can do their best work if they are worried that their mum is cold.

9.3. The payoff

If these basics are right, you won't get any prizes, or any credit. You will just avoid the penalty of not getting them wrong. What I've noticed is that getting these things wrong tends to upset your best people the most – I guess they have high working standards and expect you to have them too. The worst of all worlds is that your best people leave grumpy, and the worst people stay and muddle on!

So make sure you get the basics right. Make sure your people feel safe and supported. Then, on those secure foundations, you can build a great place to work.

A few great questions

1. Have you created a working environment where your people feel supported and safe?

2. Do you offer your staff training in stress management?

3. Are you sure all your people understand the things they can do to build resilience?

4. Are you absolutely sure that all your managers create healthy working relationships within their teams? How do you know? Do you ask their staff?

5. Are you sure your salaries are at market rate or just slightly above that?

6. Is your working environment the best you can make it?

7. What do you do to help your people remain physically and mentally healthy?

8. Do you have administrative policies that you know cause grief? Can they be simplified or changed to be more user friendly?

Rule 10:
Make it a great place to work!

We've set ourselves a goal: to be the best place in the world to work!

This is important. Remember the markets we compete in – the market for clients and the market for talent. By attracting and retaining great people, we will do great work and that will attract better clients and that in turn will help us attract even better talent… that wonderful victorious cycle.

So when we've made sure we've got the basics right, what makes a law firm a great place for our people? What makes people happy at work? There's a massive amount of research on this topic. Positive psychology is a booming industry.

10.1. The research

No apology for all these reading references here – this stuff is so important! If you understand and provide the things that make people happy at work your best people will not want to leave.

Maslow said that once we feel safe and we feel we belong, we then need 'esteem' – self-esteem, confidence, achievement, the respect of others. For most of us, work is the place where these needs can be met.

Ryan and Deci explored our desire to work further with their 'Self-Determination Theory',[22] which is about the choices people make when they're free of external influences – their intrinsic motivation. They suggest that, as humans, we're naturally curious, vital and self-motivated. We have an inherent tendency towards growth and development. In other words, we work because we want to! And we have needs to develop this tendency – the need for autonomy (when we can behave in accordance with our values and interests), competence (when we feel we're doing a good job) and relatedness (when we feel cared for and connected to others). When these needs are met, it fosters wellbeing, good health, cognitive development and social development.

As previously mentioned, Herzberg[23] identified factors that are 'motivators' relating to the work itself, and include more challenging work, recognition for achievement, opportunity to do something meaningful, and opportunity for advancement.

In Part Two of his brilliant book *Drive*,[24] Daniel Pink suggests we crave autonomy, mastery and purpose.

In *The Happiness Advantage*[25] Shawn Achor suggests that we become more successful when we're happier – and not, as so many of us think, the other way around. Our brains are hard-wired to perform at their best when we're feeling positive. Happiness is the joy we feel striving to reach our potential.

It is absolutely clear that if you provide an environment where people can feel happy and free and have meaningful and challenging work they will perform at their best.

So what can we do to provide this?

10.2. Meaning

We all want to feel our lives are meaningful – to believe we're making a contribution to the world. It's a basic part of being human. People joined your organisation because they believed in the core ideology – the reason why your business exists. They chose their area of work because it was meaningful to them. You need to keep reminding them of that. Keep reminding them how valuable their job is – how it improves your clients' lives – it is easy to forget this when bogged down in the day-to-day work. It is important for everyone. When passing a trial bundle to the support team for copying, take time to remind them why the job is important: 'Thanks for doing this. It's so important because we act for people who've suffered the most devastating injuries, and the quality of those copies is critical when they get their day in court. A great trial bundle with clear, well-paginated copies is essential for getting the judge on our side from day one.'

10.3. Freedom, trust and autonomy

I believe that people come to work to do their best and that generally they're able to make good decisions about how to do that. They neither want nor need to be micromanaged. They can be trusted to work hard because they want to.

One of my biggest successes ever has been our flexible working policy – I believe it's the most flexible in the world! It dates back to 2003, when I started it as an experiment. The policy is simple – our people can work when, where and how they like, to suit them and their clients. There are a few restrictions to make sure key roles are covered during office hours, and that we comply with the law, but we try to minimise these. It applies to holidays too. We don't track holidays – we trust people to take the right amount (but we do check in once a year to make sure they have taken at least the statutory minimum). We've never looked back. In truth, this was just formalising the way our best people had worked for years. We don't regard this as a 'staff benefit' – it works both ways. We expect our staff to be flexible to suit clients, and we want to be flexible to suit our staff. It's fine to leave to pick the children up from school at 3pm, or to go to the hairdresser on a Wednesday morning, as long as clients are happy and other goals are met. Similarly if a client needs an evening appointment we expect it to be provided. In 2014, when Virgin announced their flexible working policy, which made front-page headlines, we just laughed – we'd been operating a much more flexible policy for 11 years by that time!

If you employ the right people, you can trust them.

10.4. Good, challenging work

Work allocation is extremely important. Lawyers want to progress and they need work allocated to them that is challenging – but not too challenging!

I hear this all the time at interview – applicants asking questions about the nature of the work and the clients. They want to be sure the role will be challenging enough so that they will be learning and progressing. It's clearly near the top of their list of priorities in seeking a new job.

I was lucky. I did my training in a firm where I was given a huge amount of responsibility for client work right from the start, yet I always felt I was properly supervised and could ask if I wasn't certain of anything. I notice this going wrong so often, with junior people being thrown in at the deep end without proper support, or great people not being challenged enough and ending up bored.

We need to make sure we train our managers to get this right. It's also really important that we create a culture where people feel comfortable asking for more challenging work or for more training or support.

10.5. Good management and support

Freedom and autonomy are important, but so is good support when needed.

Lawyers want to be supported by their managers. They want senior people to be available to discuss difficult points of law. They want to feel they can call their manager late at night, if that's when they need the help. They need a relationship with their manager such that they can discuss anything that's holding them back.

Good people want to be managed. They want to have a skilled manager who will work with them to set good goals. They want to be told if they're falling short in any area. They want to be praised and recognised when they have done well. They want to have regular meetings with their manager – at least monthly – to discuss how they are and what they're working on.

Good people want to have formal appraisals. I think appraisals are really important – they're an opportunity, just once a year, to reflect on the past and to plan for the future. A good process is essential: I like the appraisee to complete a written self-appraisal first (a good form will guide the process). This allows the manager to see the appraisee's self-perception of where they are. The manager can then add his own view, and any feedback obtained from others. I suggest to our managers that each appraisal should take around a full day of their time – including the written work and the meeting. Surely every member of staff deserves such thought just once each year. The golden rule for appraisals is that there should be no surprises – if there are any problems these should have already been raised in regular one-to-one meetings. The appraisal is for summarising the year just gone, recognising what has been learnt and is still to be built on and planning the year to come.

Support is particularly important when someone makes a mistake – and we all make mistakes. It's critical that people believe they'll be supported. If they believe this, they'll speak up early, meaning there's a much better chance of a more experienced person putting the mistake right before further damage is done. Even if the mistake can't be corrected, a good manager will offer a shoulder to cry on and offer support to keep the matter in perspective thus perhaps preventing many sleepless nights.

Make sure people are not afraid to ask. I always say there's no such thing as a stupid question – just a stupid person who fails to ask it. Encourage questions!

10.6. Working only with great people

As Herzberg suggests, the wrong colleagues can be demotivating, but my observations are that having great colleagues makes people very happy. To give our clients the best service, we need to work in teams. People like to work with others who they know and trust. People like to work with those whose work they respect – they want to learn. Many times, I've watched a slightly stale team flourish when we've made a couple of really good recruits into it.

Great lawyers want to receive guidance and training from managers they respect – both for their legal skills and their management abilities. Great lawyers want to have junior people in their team to whom they can delegate work with confidence. They want to help bring on good juniors, but they don't want to waste time on those who are not committed.

10.7. Legal training

Good people are ambitious. They want to progress and they know that learning new skills is important.

The Centre for Creative Leadership[26] – an organisation founded to improve leadership worldwide – suggested that the ideal ratio for learning is 70% challenging assignments, 20% developmental relationships and 10% coursework and training. From my experience, this seems very likely to be true – good work allocation, a good line manager and some classroom learning are important in roughly these proportions.

Daniel Pink says we all want mastery. One of my favourite questions to our people is 'What do you want to be famous for?' Training provides the opportunity to master our chosen area. Have a generous budget for formal training. Allow your people to develop their interests and move towards mastery of their own subject.

10.8. Management training

Legal skills are not the only ones that are important for career progression. A great place to work will offer training in negotiating skills, people management skills, public speaking, networking, media training, social media training, personal development, personal branding, resilience, coaching... the list is endless. Have fun with this – these are all great integrating mechanisms.

Even better than insisting on people receiving training in these areas is encouraging them to give training. Lots of people find these things interesting and being asked to give training is often perceived as a public recognition of their skills.

10.9. It's who you know!

Good people understand the importance of creating their own networks. Encourage *all* your people to do this.

Most of us don't find networking easy – but like most things it is a skill and can be learnt. I think it is really important that even the most junior lawyers are encouraged to build their network of contacts. This is a life-long project. Good solid relationships built in the early years may not yield much in the way of referrals of work – but as you and your contacts rise through your respective organisations opportunities for referrals will increase.

10.10. Great infrastructure

People will think twice about leaving a firm with amazing infrastructure. A firm where there are top professionals to advise them on compliance and HR issues, where meeting rooms are available and good coffee is offered to their clients. People really do value having the best IT systems, good case management, accessible from anywhere in the world. They value having a great laptop and phone.

The more you can do to build and maintain an infrastructure like this, the more likely your best people are to stay.

10.11. Fun together

I think it's really important that your people have fun together, both in and out of the daily work. Spending time together and getting to know each other builds trust. It gives opportunities to remind each other about purpose and values. It provides great integrating mechanisms. There's absolutely no downside, apart from a relatively small financial spend.

Fun in work includes great debate on legal topics, discussing innovative ways to run cases, and strategy or marketing away-days with the whole team.

Out of work, the world is your oyster! Think parties (lots of them), ad hoc celebrations of a big win, physical challenges (a marathon, the three peaks) and fun days (crystal maze, wine tasting, theatre club). One of our biggest successes in the fun category, 'the firm walk' came from my school days. Sometimes in the summer term the headmaster would announce in assembly, 'Today we are going on a walk! Lessons are cancelled. Go and get changed and meet in the playground in 15 minutes.' He'd then lead the whole school on a full day's walk in the North York Moors with a picnic lunch. I have such fond memories of those walks that I decided to do the same for our firm!

10.12. Generational differences

I don't believe generational differences should be a serious issue in the workplace. Perhaps a controversial view as so much is written about how the generations are different. I'm not denying that different generations have different expectations – they were shaped by the world they grew up in. But we're all people, and people haven't changed that much in the last few thousand years.

It's said that Generation X (born 1961–1980) are very concerned with work–life balance. But wouldn't we all like this? Generation

Y, the 'Millennials' (1981–1995), have a reputation for being concerned with freedom and flexibility – but, again, don't we all want this? As a baby-boomer (1945–1960), I'm told that I should be concerned with job security, and that Generation Z (born after 1995), will want the same. But as humans, we all want this – it's just a form of safety. It may be true that the Millennials worry about job security less – but they still prefer a job move to be their own choice.

What has changed is the use of technology – if you want to attract and retain the best Millennials and increasingly the Zillennials (born post 1995) who are just beginning to enter the work force you will need to have the very best IT systems. And don't forget your millennial clients will demand this too! New staff will expect to be able to apply for a job from an app on their phone and clients will expect to be able to examine progress on their matter in the same way.

IT investment is just going to get more and more important.

A few great questions

1. Do you regularly remind your people about why the work they do is important? Can you think of more ways this could be done?

2. Do you offer the flexibility that people seek to make their job a better fit with their life? Can you think of ways of doing this that would benefit your staff and your clients?

3. Do you have strong systems for work allocation – to make sure everyone is stretched a little so that they are growing – but not so much that they get stressed and ill?

4. Do you take management training for all those who manage others very seriously?

5. Do all your managers truly buy into the need to invest in their people and allocate significant time to appraisals and management meetings?

6. Do you offer wide-ranging training – not just on the law but on management skills too?

7. Do you have a long-term strategy for upgrading your IT to keep up with the demands of future generations?

Rule 11:
People crave recognition and reward

We all enjoy recognition. When we complete a marathon, we love being given the medal to wear around our necks. When we see a celebrity being given a knighthood, we can see their pride. When we're admitted as a solicitor, we're proud of our achievement, the recognition of many years of study.

At work, when we recognise the success of colleagues, it makes them feel good. The act of recognition triggers the release of the happy brain chemicals serotonin and oxytocin and we feel love, trust, pride – we feel that others like and respect us. This makes us feel strong and confident and able to continue to do our best work.

But human motivation is a complex thing. We all like setting goals for ourselves and achieving them. When I decided I wanted to run a marathon I was totally committed and motivated to reach that goal. But we don't like others setting goals for us – I can imagine what I would have said if someone had *told* me to run a marathon!

We know from Rule 10 that people have their own intrinsic motivation, and we explored how we can support that at work. So the next question is how do we design systems for reward and recognition that will build even further on that intrinsic motivation and encourage people to do their best work?

11.1. Carrots and sticks don't work!

There is overwhelming evidence that for creative work – the sort of work that people have intrinsic motivation to do – carrots and sticks ('IF you do this, THEN I will pay you this') do not work! In fact, they stifle creativity.

Daniel Pink explains why this is so in his book *Drive*.[27] He talks through study after study that show people do creative work better when they do it because they want to rather than because they've been told that if they do it well, they'll get some sort of reward. In short, Daniel Pink suggests that carrots and sticks can extinguish intrinsic motivation; diminish performance; crush creativity; crowd out good behaviour; encourage cheating, shortcuts and unethical behaviour; become addictive; and foster short-term thinking. When one of the core values of the firm is 'firm first', i.e. firm before self (demonstrated by behaviours such as passing work to the right person and supporting colleagues when needed), it is easy to see how damaging carrots and sticks can be to the organisation culture.

Of course, not all work needs creativity – sometimes you just need people to muck in and do a boring task e.g. help with an office move. In these circumstances, Daniel Pink suggests, a reward can help. Explain why the task is necessary, acknowledge that it's boring and allow people to do it in their own way. Offer a reward for those who help.

11.2. What you measure is what you get

I have observed this well-known adage to be true time and time again! What you measure for an individual influences how they behave.

Take the old chestnut of 'chargeable hours'. Personally, I believe that nothing has been more damaging to the legal profession than charging clients by the hour... but let me leave that hobby horse to one side, because until there are changes in the law about how legal bills are assessed by the court in litigation, we're stuck with it! To be clear, I do believe that lawyers need to record how much time they spend on a client matter. Not, however, for the purpose of charging the client, but for the purpose of knowing whether or not a job has been profitable!

When the focus is put on chargeable hours logged, they go up. I have watched this happen time and time again.

When the focus is put on realisation ratio (chargeable hours logged divided by fees billed) chargeable hours go down and realisation ratio goes up – because lawyers soon grasp that one way to get better realisation is just to record fewer hours!

We need to make really sure we're measuring the right things. What is important for financial measures is that we give the clients the most value for our hours. So we need to find ways to encourage people to record accurately (no padding and no shaving) the time they spend AND encourage them to find innovative solutions so that the amount of time is as low as possible for the biggest value to the client. In other words, we need to reward *accurate* recording of time spent *and* realisation ratio.

So what is it really important to measure? The answer to that will vary according to the firm strategy.

It was way back in the 1990s that I came up with our five key metrics:

- Exceeding client expectations

- Taking management and administrative duties seriously

- Financial performance – hours recorded, realisation ratio, fees collected

- Practice development success – activities engaged in and value of work brought in

- Firm contribution – all-round 'good eggness'

We measure whether we've exceeded client expectations by asking our clients. The results have been on the Bolt Burdon website since 2004. Every lawyer has goals for the percentage of questionnaires returned and the percentage of those where clients expectations were exceeded.

All-round 'good eggness' is important to us because of the sort of firm we want to be – a firm where we work in teams and our loyalty is to the whole firm. If someone drafts a good precedent, we want it to be shared firm wide. If someone lands a great new client, we want them to introduce the new client to their colleagues.

These measures are now deeply embedded in our culture, although if I were to fix them now, I'd put the financial measures last –

because I firmly believe that good financial results are really just the consequence of doing the other things well.

11.3. People like to have goals

Edwin Locke has been studying the power of goal-setting since the late 1960s. He suggests goals are motivating and goals that are both specific and difficult lead to the highest performance. Goals should also be important to the individual and be considered achievable.[28]

My own observations are that people find clear goals really helpful. Everyone wants to know what is expected of them. I believe that it is important when goal-setting to *agree* the goals – not impose them.

As mentioned in Rule 5, there are outcome goals (a specific end result) and process goals (a regular behaviour that will result in an outcome). We already know that autonomy is important. So good work goals are outcome goals, leaving the individual to decide how to achieve them where possible. I am a huge believer in setting SMART goals (Specific, Measurable, Achievable, Relevant and Timed). As I said in Rule 5, a SMART goal is easy to recognise – there will be a day sometime in the future where you can ask yourself, 'Did I achieve my goal?' – the answer will be 'Yes' or 'No'. So do agree SMART goals with all of your people. It gives great clarity as to where you want their time to be focused in the months ahead.

Process goals sometimes won't be connected to an outcome, but rather daily habits that you want to develop and keep for life. These may be the most effective goals of all – for if something can become a habit, it will become something you do unconsciously and will not need willpower to keep it going. Setting outcome goals for things that you want to continue forever is a mistake often made – this is one of the reasons why diets don't work. We set an outcome goal – to eat certain things until we weigh X, then as soon as we achieve that weight, we go straight back to our old eating habits and the weight goes back on.

Be really careful that the goals are the right ones. Remember: what you measure is what you get.

11.4. Praise

I think one of the best, and most simple, management books of all time is *The One Minute Manager*.[29] A 'one-minute manager' does one-minute goal-setting, one-minute praising and one-minute re-directs. To ensure lots of praising he walks around looking for people doing something right and gives them 'a one-minute praising' – telling them what they did right, how good that makes him feel and how it helps the team. This allows them to feel the praise and then encourages more of the same behaviours. People love praise – but only if they think it's really deserved.

Praise from the most senior partners is even more special than from the line manager! I know I have a reputation for having very high expectations – I don't give praise very often, but I know that when I do, it's really appreciated. I wish I'd spent more time walking around looking for people doing things right!

11.5. Recognition

Even more special than one-to-one praising is giving public recognition to people who have done things right. There are hundreds of ways this can be done – a mention at a meeting, an impromptu trip to the pub to celebrate a success, an unexpected bottle of wine left on the desk...

It was probably about 1992 that we invented our 'Weekend in Paris Award'. Roger and I were in a meeting with some important clients. The meeting was intense and after about an hour we called for more coffee. Jackie, our receptionist at the time, brought in coffee beautifully presented as trained. Then as she was passing the cups around, she spilled some coffee in my saucer. 'Oh, I'm so sorry. Let me get you another one,' she said. 'No, don't worry,' I replied. The meeting was important and I was keen to get back to it. So Jackie left the room. A minute later, she came back with a clean saucer. We were very impressed and so was our client who said 'I wish we had a receptionist who cared like yours'. Jackie cared – she wanted the coffee to be perfect. That was exactly the sort of dedication we wanted from our people. That Christmas, we presented our very first Paris trip to Jackie – yes, a weekend for two in Paris for not settling for a dirty saucer!

The 'Weekend in Paris Award' lives on, and we now also have its baby sister, the 'Extra Miler Award' – dinner for two at a really nice restaurant.

External recognition is also important. Many people see external qualifications as recognition that they have attained a new level. This must be a good thing. Encourage your people to get more qualifications and support them in it. It's good for them and good for your firm, too. A generous training budget is seen as a real benefit by staff.

11.6. Promotion

A clear promotion structure is an important way of giving public recognition. We got this wrong when we first started Bolt Burdon. We didn't think 'status' was important – in fact, we were rather against it. But eventually our staff persuaded us that it was important to them and so we fell into line and we now have a very clear promotion structure. To get promoted you need to have performed to a defined level in each of our five key areas (exceeding client expectations, management and admin, financial performance, practice development and good eggness).

I now understand why this is important – back to the brain science and those tribes! We like to know where we fit in the hierarchy in our tribe – this is hard wired within us – it's part of our social safety mechanism. We want to know who can tell us what to do and who we can call upon to give us help and support.

Millennials regard rapid career progression as particularly important – they want to see themselves moving up and getting a better title, more money and the opportunity to grow further. They want to see internal promotions over external hires.[30] Keep them happy with lots of steps on your promotion ladder.

And of course, a promotion is always a cause for public recognition – bring out the Champagne!

11.7. Bonuses

Boy, did we get this wrong!

I don't really know how it happened, but for some years we fell into the trap of paying bonuses calculated as a percentage of fees billed over target. A classic 'if-then' sort of bonus scheme. And then we wondered why we were seeing behaviours of hoarding work, not passing cases on even though clients were suffering delays, only taking cases where fees were likely to be high, reluctance to do any training or marketing… and in a firm where what we really value is delighting clients, teamwork and practice development.

It was reading *Drive*[31] that finally pulled us back on track! We realised that we were rewarding one of our five measures above all the others – which was interpreted internally as us saying it is really only fees billed that matter. That was not the truth – all five measures are important.

I do think bonuses are important – ones that say 'thank you' for good behaviours and achievements. We still love giving big bonuses to those who have achieved excellence in any one of our five key areas. We do let people know we have a 'bonus pot' and how the size of the pot is calculated. When the firm is doing well because we're seeing lots of the right behaviours, we take huge pleasure in awarding big 'thank you' bonuses to those who have contributed to that.

A few great questions

1. Are you stifling intrinsic motivation by paying if-then bonuses?

2. Are you clear about the behaviours that may trigger a bonus as a thank you for great contribution?

3. Do you have a clear range of measures that cover the behaviours and results you seek?

4. Does everyone in your organisation have clear goals – both outcome and process?

5. Do you have a clear promotion structure – with lots of rungs if possible?

6. Do you have lots and lots of public ways of recognising things done right?

Rule 12:
Choose your partners more carefully than your spouse!

In most small law firms, the equity partners are the business owners – they finance the firm, make the big decisions together and their income depends on the firm making a profit.

The partners have bound their financial futures together – they will all sink or swim together. They've committed to spending time together and nurturing the firm together. A dishonest partner can bring them all down. They will usually have their houses on the line supporting bank borrowing. In extreme business failure, they will all become bankrupt together.

When you offer someone a partnership in your firm, you're saying, 'I trust you with my reputation, with my livelihood, with all my assets and I completely believe that you care about this business as much as I do.' That is a huge commitment.

It was a former partner of mine who advocated that you should choose your business partners more carefully than your spouse. He was right! A partnership dispute is even more messy than a divorce – I know, I've done both!

Choose carefully who you want to be in business with.

12.1. What is a 'partner'?

There's a fundamental problem with the word 'partner' as it can be used to describe a great lawyer at the top of their profession but who may just be a salaried employee, and an owner of the business, so it's always important to be clear what you mean. In this Rule, I'm talking about the business owners – equity partners – the people who fund the business and share the profits or losses.

I believe there is a place for a salaried partner – an employee who has the title 'partner' because they're a great lawyer. Clients like to deal with partners, and people like the status of the title – that's all fine. A good lawyer can be a salaried partner for life, or as a step on their way up to equity.

For many years, Roger and I – the founding partners – were the only true equity partners in our firm. We always knew we'd have to bring in new partners or face a merger or sale before we could retire. We didn't want to sell out on our dreams – we wanted our legacy to live on – we wanted to pass our business on to people who believed what we believed, so that it would continue to grow and flourish long after we'd gone. We knew we had to find the right people to share our business with.

Salaried partners came and went, but we just weren't getting it right. We even made a couple of offers of equity, but they were refused – there was a perception that it was 'Roger and Lynne's firm' and that would never change. I am delighted to say they were wrong.

12.2. Wrong turns

We made many mistakes along the way. We lost our first two potential equity partners when they were made an offer they couldn't refuse by a much bigger firm. A little later, an excellent lawyer turned out to have absolutely no appetite for risk – he would have held back our growth. One man we liked very much left after a disagreement over money – it became clear he'd be better suited in a firm where partners are paid on an 'eat what you kill' basis i.e. are rewarded for their own personal billings, which was not our way. We even had two very good potential equity partners at one time – but the problem there was they didn't like each other! It was such a shame, but I knew we could only offer one of them a seat at our table and we were forced to choose. The other one soon left us. It's critical that partners want to spend time together and for that they need to like each other.

Mistakes are painful but must be borne. Over the years, we've had to call upon our partnership deed a few times to expel a partner who was not performing in some way. This was very difficult, as these were people we really liked. We really wanted them as partners. This is where the leader must take the lead and tackle the matter head on. Usually it's enough to invite the partner to leave – but if an expulsion vote is necessary, so be it.

We've always had a very tough expulsion policy in our partnership deed – an equity partner can be expelled on one month's notice without any reason. We always discuss this carefully with our new partners, but I believe that the harshness of the expulsion clause is a fair price to pay for knowing that a non-performing partner can be expelled very quickly and thus minimise damage to the business. The firm, of course, can always offer more generous departure terms if that feels right in the circumstances. As with everything, it must always be 'firm first'.

12.3. Make sure partners really want to be partners!

The partnership model is often difficult for people outside the profession to understand. As I approach retirement, it's often assumed that I'll be able to sell my share in the business. When I explain that there's no sale – that when a partner leaves, they get nothing for the value of the business they have helped to grow – there's often surprise. But this is the very essence of the partnership model. As Stephen Mayson[32] says, 'ownership' is a mirage. The partners are not so much the owners but the custodians of the business. It makes sense when you think about it. There's very little in a law firm that can be owned: some capital assets; some firm-specific systems; some contacts and records perhaps – but the vast majority of the value of a law firm lives in the heads of the lawyers. It's not possible to own people – they vote for themselves to stay or walk at any time. Restrictive covenants can help protect relationships with clients, but clients will only stay if you have the right lawyers.

I have no doubt that most of the value of the firm at any time lies in the ability of the partners to create a firm where the best lawyers want to work, and therefore is one that great clients want to instruct. When a partner walks out the door, they're no longer a part of this.

Partnership is a hard-fought prize. You'll have invested a great deal in the business in terms of your time and energy before you get a partnership share. If you're good enough to make the grade, the existing partners give you a profit share in the business as a reward for what you've done so far, and in the belief that while you're a partner you'll continue to improve the firm in some way. When you leave, you take your talents with you and leave your profit share behind.

This model is under challenge, as many firms seek to limit liability and change the ownership model to Limited Liability Partnerships and Limited Companies. We've debated a change many times, but I remain a fan of the traditional partnership, where all partners know that there's no safety net. This is sometimes considered an old-fashioned view and it may be that, in the not-too-distant future, my firms will change their structure. I hope that can be done without changing the fundamental essence of our partnership.

One reason the traditional partnership model works incredibly well for small law firms is because the model is not attractive to employee-minded partners. As a business owner your income is not certain. There have been a couple of years since we founded our firm in which we have made a loss and then we have had to borrow money in order to pay the partners cash to live on. There have also been many years where my income has been more than I ever dreamt of. That's the game. You only get paid if you succeed, and the whole team fails or succeeds together.

I also believe that if team-working is the most important thing – and I do believe that – then profits should be shared with the same deal for every partner. I've heard all the arguments as to why the managing partner should get more, why a super-performing partner should get a bonus share, and the discussions about bonus pools or profit shares, but I just don't believe this works to the overall advantage in a small firm. So much time would be spent discussing how to share profits every year and there's bound to be resentment somewhere. The thing that makes the partnership successful is the understanding that all equity partners make an equal contribution but each in their own way.

When we're thinking of admitting new partners, I like to think in terms of cake. At present, we're baking a nice cake and we'll each get a slice (profit share). If we bring in a new partner, we'll need to divide the cake into more slices. So I ask whether that partner will contribute to baking a bigger cake, so resulting in more cake for everyone. Remembering that the bar should be raised with every hire, it seems to me that this is a very good test – never forgetting that there are many ways that a new partner can contribute to the cake baking.

12.4. Be certain the new partner shares the business 'why'

There's no place in any partnership for a partner who is not totally committed to the 'core ideology' – the reason the business exists. Remember this can never change, so anyone who does not completely agree with it from the start will never be happy in the firm. Sooner or later, this mismatch will end in tears and possibly a partnership dispute.

This is unlikely to be a problem if you've been really clear in explaining the core ideology of the business because potential partners will, to a large extent, self-select. Who would want to work in a firm where the 'why' was not meaningful to them? But there are a few people who are motivated more by money than by meaning. If the firm is successful, a partnership may be attractive to them for that reason. Do not let such a person in.

12.5. A shared vision

Even if partners really like each other and share the core ideology, that's not enough. For the business to work, they must have similar views on risk, appetite for borrowing, work ethic, and short-term and long-term earnings expectations.

That was one of our biggest lessons in our previous firm – we were hungry, we wanted to work harder and take more risks to earn more, but our partners were already content with what they had. There is no right or wrong, but if partners don't agree on the degree of risk or the amount of commitment expected, it will end in dispute.

These things can, to some extent, be examined in a partnership assessment process. You won't even be talking about a partnership for anyone who doesn't have an appetite for hard work, for example. But it's very hard to really find out about someone's appetite for borrowing and risk. This is where a period acting 'as if' really comes into its own. The prospective partner is invited to join partners' meetings and participate in discussions exactly 'as if' they were a partner. When a decision actually has to be made about borrowing £1m to invest in a new practice management system, or signing a new ten-year lease for the business, that's when you'll really find out what makes a partner tick.

12.6. Home-grown is always best

Appointing a new partner who's been with the firm for some time is always going to be less risky than appointing someone from outside the firm. You will be confident that such a person shares the core ideology and values.

However, sometimes, it's necessary to fill a top-level vacancy and bring a new person into the firm at a senior level. If this is the case, bring them in as a salaried partner – even if it's at a very high salary – until you're completely confident that this is a person you want to be in business with.

12.7. Partners do not have to be solicitors

Solicitors do have a lot in common. From our first days at law school, we're drilled in solicitors' ethics and have had common training. However, I really believe that a firm can be even stronger with other professions around the table – provided they share the core ideology. We've had as equity partners a financial advisor and a costs lawyer. I would love to see an HR director or an IT director in our partnerships. The qualification is not the point – there are just two questions to consider:

- Do they share our core ideology, values and vision?

- Will they help us bake that bigger cake?

12.8. Entrepreneurs

It's likely that you're considering someone for equity partnership because they already play a valuable role in the business, probably as a great lawyer and probably as they have some skills as a manager and business developer. As an equity partner, that's not enough.

For someone to be admitted to the equity, I need to be convinced that their contribution will make me richer in some way – in money or pride or whatever else I desire! So a new equity partner needs to be an entrepreneur. They need to bring something to the partnership that is unique to them, something that's new or that will build on what we already have in a way that no one else can.

There are many ways this can be achieved. A partner could make their contribution by: developing an area of work you couldn't do without them; servicing a type of client you don't already service; being constantly innovative with new ways of working that will result in greater efficiency; being exceptionally skilled at managing key client relationships; being skilled at managing people in a way that will result in better staff retention.

Sometimes, being a partner in a small firm is thought to be for those who couldn't make it in the global giants. I strongly disagree. Small or large is just a choice – both have advantages and disadvantages. In small firms, all the partners must be real entrepreneurs. Together they make the decisions about where the firm is going. Being a partner in a small firm is fun. A partners' dinner with the people I've hand-picked to work with is one of the things I enjoy most in life.

12.9. How do we slice the cake?

I believe in keeping this very simple. The job of the partners is to work together to bake a bigger cake. The key is to keep all partners focused on that – and not to waste precious time and energy on discussions about how big each partner's slice should be. Any partner not fully contributing to the bake should be expelled – don't even think of offering a reduced partnership share for reduced contribution.

It is important to remember that partners are being paid for three different things and I think it is wise to separate these in allocating profit share:

- Interest on capital contributed – this is the return for investing money in the business. Partners will often choose to retain their own money in the firm rather than rely on bank borrowings.

- A 'notional salary' – this is the reward for working in the business – a sum equivalent to what you might pay an employee doing the same job. I think it is important to identify this sum so that you can see the 'real profit'.

- After deduction of interest and notional salary you are left with 'real profit' – the reward for taking and managing the risk – for being an entrepreneur. This will be divided in the profit-sharing proportions however you choose to calculate those.

12.10. What about retirement?

When partners arrive, that is the time to agree the time of departure. At the time of writing, age discrimination laws are still uncertain for partnerships but, subject to these, I believe that it's in the best interests of the firm that there is an agreed retirement date for partners. We chose age 65, and as a person getting very close to that age now, that feels about right. It's critical to make way for younger partners to keep the firm fresh and relevant. Of course the age can always be varied if it suits both parties.

Retirement isn't easy. I helped ease Roger through his very successfully, and now I'm facing mine. For most professionals, work is a serious part of their identity and when that's suddenly taken away, it's easy to feel bereft and useless.

Retirement may be even harder for founders. Founders tend to have even more investment in the business. Luke Johnson summed it up:

> 'For a founder, running a business is not the same as any other job. It's likely to be an all-consuming passion, a whirlwind, an obsession and a high stakes game. It's more than just their work and their fortune – it's their identity and their life purpose.'[33]

One bad day, I described my own succession planning as 'digging my own grave'. Partners need support at this time. We support them on the way in, and it's important to offer support on the way out, too. What that may look like will be different for everyone.

I've had a lot of support from my partners, and now I've stood down as managing partner, I've created a really exciting role for myself doing coaching, facilitating and training for our partners and staff.

12.11. Don't forget a partnership deed

It shouldn't be necessary to say this, but I fear it is! You *must* have a partnership deed recording the terms agreed.

It's not comfortable to think about, but the deed is the document that will keep things as fair as possible if it all goes wrong. So draft it on the assumption you're all falling out with each other. With any luck you'll never get it out of the drawer.

12.12. When we get it right

We made some wrong turns but eventually we found the right people. We now have really strong equity partners around the table in both firms. We also have people waiting in the wings who would love to join the club – good people. Our future is safe.

When you get it right, the firm will thrive.

A few great questions

1. Are you clear about your own expectations about risk, borrowing, reward and desire to work hard?

2. Are you happy about your current choice of partners knowing that your financial futures are dependent on each other? If not, what are you going to do about it?

3. Are you happy about your governance and profit-sharing regime, and the behaviours they're encouraging?

4. When do you expect your partners to retire? Do you have a plan to help them with that?

5. Do you have an up-to-date partnership deed?

Rule 13:
It's good to cry in partners' meetings

It's only in recent years that I've learnt the huge value of a strong 'top team' – the group of people that are responsible for running the firm. In most small firms, including ours, that's the equity partners.

To make this group strong you need to work hard at it. Commit to giving time and energy to building a strong team.

13.1. Where my rule came from

For a long time, the top team consisted of only me and Roger – the two founding partners. We were a very strong team. We discussed top-level strategy, but other than that, Roger's main leadership role was as my sounding board and shoulder to cry on! He was passionate about the clients and the cases, and was happy to leave the day-to-day leadership and management to me.

I didn't know any other way and took on all the responsibility – I grew very broad shoulders.

When we took on our first full equity partners my world changed completely. Suddenly, other people were entitled to a say – and sometimes they didn't agree with me! At first our meetings were not good. Sometimes I assumed they were just a formality (me trying to gain approval for a decision I'd already made) and other times simply a platform for those who shouted loudest to get their own way.

I had always invested a lot of my time meeting other managing partners and learning about life in other firms. I'd heard their tales of woe about the problems they had managing their partners. I'd heard of maverick partners who would say nothing in meetings then leave the meeting and tell anyone who'd listen that they didn't agree with the decision made. I'd heard of factions – two or three groups of partners who'd had 'pre-meetings' and arrived determined to win the day. Perhaps worst of all, there were those who'd taken a seat at the table but made no positive contribution whatsoever.

I began to realise how important it was to create a strong leadership team, where all the partners felt equally important, where we could have good debate and decision making and where tasks and decisions that did not justify all partners could be delegated with trust.

After some thought I put together an equity partner development programme – one day each month out of the office for two years. These days were so successful that we kept them going although we only have about six a year now. We use the days for formal training, team-building exercises and anything big that needs resolution.

My rule 'It's good to cry in partners' meetings' was discovered following a very ugly incident in a restaurant after one of these partner away-days. It was a very difficult time for me – Roger, who'd been my partner for over 30 years, was nearing retirement. I was working hard to build relationships with my new partners and I knew this was essential if we were to continue being a successful partnership. A few weeks before the meeting, I'd discovered that Roger and two of the newer partners had been out together for dinner – and had not invited me. I'd spoken to Roger about it and he'd assured me it had just been a social event – but I was not convinced – it made no sense – why would they want Roger at a social event and not me? I was the one that was going to be their partner going forward. I wasn't the only partner they had not invited but I just did not understand why they had invited Roger and not invited me, or indeed the others. I was trying to let it go but something came up at that dinner – I really can't remember what now – and I was triggered. The red mist descended, and suddenly, all the emotion I was bottling up came out. I was angry and very upset. Through my tears I tried to explain why I was so upset but I am not at all sure I succeeded.

Reflecting back now it is clear to me what had happened. I was feeling lonely and vulnerable at the time because Roger was retiring. Would it work with the new partners? Would I be able to build the same relationship with them as I had with Roger? Would my voice continue to matter? Would I still have my sounding board and shoulder to cry on – essential support for a managing partner? Understanding the brain science helps. My amygdala had been on full alert, looking for threat in the changing circumstances. My anterior cingulate cortex had identified that I had been excluded from the gang – panic stations! Fight, flight or freeze – I chose to fight!

But what really matters is that I learnt something very important. For a partnership to be strong, partners have to be able to discuss everything – not just business matters, but anything that may affect their relationship with each other. It has to be OK to cry, scream, laugh and show every sort of emotion in a partners' meeting because these are normal human behaviours that arise in every close human relationship. A group of partners is like a family – and no one would want to be part of a family where emotions were not shared. It has to be OK to show vulnerability – that is what makes the team strong.

We've had many other emotional incidents since – rows over wedding invitations, who should manage whom, individual bonuses and individual partners' contributions. I'm proud to say that we were able to allow the tears and tantrums, discuss what happened and then move forward. With each such incident, the team gets stronger. We have continued to work hard on our relationships and I now have a very strong bond with all my new partners in both firms. We are truly a team.

13.2. Why a strong top team is important

I now have absolutely no doubt that the strength of the top team is one of the most important factors in the success of a business. The relevant word is 'team'. The top team needs to work together towards a common goal – the vision!

If every member of the team is completely committed to doing whatever it takes to work with each other to deliver the vision, and to work together to bake a bigger cake for the benefit of all then that will make a very strong team and thus a very successful firm.

13.3. Who's in the top team?

We are small enough that the top team is all the equity partners. As I mentioned earlier, a team works best when it's family sized. This is so that the whole team can sit around a table and chat – rather like a family over dinner.

The magic of a small partnership is that the big decision-makers are the entrepreneurs, those who have committed their futures together, so everyone has the same desired outcome. Others may be consulted and even contribute to top team meetings – accountants, other group leaders, professional managers – but by invitation only. The big decisions are made by the equity partners.

13.4. Know, like and trust each other

For a top team to be strong, everyone in it must like and trust each other. And it's impossible to like or trust anyone unless you know them. So the way to start building a strong top team is to do lots and lots of things to encourage the partners to get to know each other. That is where the partner away-days come in – full days away from the office to get to know each other and to discuss the big issues with the luxury of time.

These big meetings have tough agendas designed to make sure we really dig deep and explore our thoughts and feelings on the difficult issues.

We have included on our agenda:

- Getting-to-know-you exercises, e.g. asking each other some personal questions: What are you most proud of? What are you ashamed of? Tell us something about you we don't know already. Tell us about your parents, your siblings and your family as you grew up.

- Looking at the differences between our MBTI[34] profiles. There was some scepticism about how helpful it could be to classify people into one of the 16 types until one of our partners read out a description of her type that she'd found on the internet. We were in hysterics – it wasn't *like* her, it *was* her!

- Debating our individual goals for the year ahead, including how much we each want to earn five years from now, and how we see that happening. Or whether we each prefer to borrow more money to grow faster.

- Asking how hard we each want to work. Do we feel we have the balance right now? Are we each doing the right work? What should we stop doing and what might we add?

- Asking who we each see as future equity partners, and what we're doing to nurture them.

- Making a presentation on how we might bake a bigger cake.

There are endless possibilities.

We've tried these meetings with an external facilitator and without – I recommend a mixture. I also think it's important that the managing partner is not expected to arrange and chair all these full-day meetings, as it's important that she's free to take part. If you have senior partners, they may be able to do this role; otherwise, partners can take turns depending on the subject matter of the day.

We always have dinner afterwards – just for fun and to make sure any wounds are healed if there have been tough debates!

13.5. Roles and responsibilities

It is important that the members of the top team are really clear about their roles and responsibilities.

The responsibility of the top team is to make the big decisions – values, strategy, vision, business plan – these are the things the top team should be discussing, not getting bogged down in day-to-day decisions. It is the responsibility of the chair to make sure this happens.

The top team needs to do regular leadership training. There is so much leadership material out there – make learning about it part of the fun. Give set reading and then discuss the books you've read together. Get on some training courses. Some partners may want to consider doing an MBA.

The top team will delegate day-to-day decision making, usually to a managing partner who, in turn, may delegate to others – perhaps a finance director or other professional managers. The managing partner is accountable to the top team – and the top team has a role in supporting the managing partner and operating as a sounding board for her.

With the right to be involved in top-level decision making comes responsibilities. A top team member needs to commit to the following:

- To contribute. It's not acceptable to just sit back and listen.

- To say what they really think! No space for 'yes men' on the top team.

- To listen. This is a team, and there must be a commitment from everyone to listen, and to ask genuine questions from a place of curiosity until they do understand what is being said and why.

- To get to know the other members of the team as people.

- To learn about leadership and management.

13.6. Listening rounds

The chair must make sure everyone contributes. One thing we've found really useful is 'listening rounds'.[35]

We use these at the start of a discussion about a big issue, with an open question. Something like, 'How's everyone feeling about this problem on our agenda?' or maybe 'What do we feel about making Jim a partner?'

The idea of the listening round is that someone volunteers to start and everyone else commits to doing nothing but listen to that person. Nothing but listen. No interruptions, no responses. Listening with the single intent of understanding what they're saying. The speaking person should have the full attention and eye contact of everyone in the room. It's OK to write one or two words down as an aide memoire for something to pick up on later, but nothing more than that. The speaker knows they will not be interrupted and that they have as much time as they need. A pause is not interpreted as the end of their turn – you wait for them to confirm they are finished. People should be encouraged to talk about their feelings as well as the facts. Emotions are welcome and, indeed, likely to improve the quality of the round. There must be no rush – the intent is to get everyone to explore and express their own thoughts and feelings.

When the first speaker has finished, they invite the person next to them to continue the round. That person then says what they want to say; the same rules apply. They can say something new, comment on what has been said already or ask questions for clarification – but those questions will not be answered until the person they're addressed to has their turn again – and only then if that person chooses to answer.

The round goes on – round and round – until no one has anything left to say.

There's no place to hide in a listening round. Everyone must contribute, everyone gets unlimited time to say what they think and everyone has time to think uninterrupted as they speak.

At the top team level, decisions are very important. Even more important is that everyone in the room is completely on board with any decision made. Nothing is more damaging to a business than partners who leave a meeting feeling disgruntled about a decision that has been made. Even if they tow the party line, they will not do it enthusiastically.

After the listening round is finished, there needs to be time for normal debate and discussion. If a decision has to be made consider the steps in my PROCEED model described in Rule 15 (Problem, Relevant facts, Options, Consult, Evaluation criteria, Evaluation of options, Decide a course of action).

13.7. Commitment

With really important decisions I like the Quaker way.[36] Everyone needs to commit to arriving at a meeting with an open mind and to looking for creative solutions. Everyone must commit to fully engaging in the process, listening for wisdom and truth and speaking their minds. The process continues until a solution or course of action emerges that everyone is ready to support and commit to – until 'the feeling of the meeting' emerges. The role of the chair is so important here; he needs to commit to actively managing the debate, making sure everyone is contributing, noticing any negative or disengaged body language and calling it out. It's impossible to get commitment to proactively supporting a decision unless everyone has really had their say.

That is how I think major decisions should be made by the top team. Yes, it is very time consuming, but remember the top team are only making very important decisions. The huge advantage is that the ultimate decision will be one that everyone in the room completely supports.

13.8. Recording the decisions

While I don't believe in keeping a detailed minute of every debate, I do think a memo recording the agreed course of action is necessary. My experience is that there's always a risk of people leaving the meeting, getting back to their desk and doing nothing – or even worse, completely forgetting that the decision has been made (OK – I'm guilty as charged!) or not properly remembering what the decision was!

13.9. Walking the talk, and talking the talk

The top team must be a shining example, to everyone in the firm, of living the values and decisions of the organisation.

It's not enough for any top team member to leave the meeting and go back to the day job, whatever that is. They must make time to talk the talk *and* walk the talk. Find ways to talk to key members of staff about the decisions that have been made and why they're important. Even more important is to demonstrate their commitment by their daily actions.

The most important thing a top team can demonstrate is the power of a strong team. If the top team is a good team, the members will pass that ethos on to other teams in the organisation they are part of.

One thing some partners find difficult is the issue of divided loyalties. In a firm where a top value is 'firm first', there can be no divided loyalty. The first loyalty must be to the top team –

because that team will always have the best interests of the whole organisation in mind. Individual members of the top team will have other interests – the interest of their own area of work or the individuals in their own work team perhaps – but these must come second to their commitment to the top team. If they cannot commit to that, they cannot be partners in our firm.

This commitment to talk the talk and walk the talk is a proactive one – it is not about keeping quiet or pretending to agree with a decision. It is recognising that, together, you made the best possible decision in the best interests of the firm, and then supporting the implementation of that decision wholeheartedly.

13.10. Accountability

The top team members are accountable to each other. The degree to which members of a team hold each other accountable is a clear indication of the strength of the team.

I think it is important to distinguish accountability as top team member from accountability in the day job. Top team members will also have a 'day job', most typically as the leader of a work group within the firm. That role will have responsibilities for line management, recruitment, delivering financial targets, etc. Usually, accountability for that role will be to the managing partner.

Top team accountability is for top team decisions and actions.

If a member of the top team sees another member fail to keep promises made, then they need to hold them to account, in person and immediately. This is not an easy thing to do, but it must be done. Some people find this very difficult indeed, but my strong advice is to kill the monster while it's a baby. The longer you leave it, the harder it will be. If you notice someone not following through on promises made in a top team meeting or not walking or talking the talk tackle it head on.

You might need to think about how best to do it – because your words may not be very welcome. But you are only doing it because you care. You care about your firm and you care about your partner. You want your partner to do what they promised. You're not serving them if you ignore what you've noticed.

You really only have two choices: mention it to the partner immediately, in private, or save it for the next top team meeting. Which of these is right probably depends on the facts. Normally I would advocate mentioning it immediately – and then hopefully the partner will be back on track before the next meeting. If not, you need to bring it up at the meeting. Where there was complete buy-in to the decision in the first place, this should not cause offence. The key thing is 'honest intent' – if your honest intent is to make sure the top team is keeping its promises then why would that cause offence?

What you should *not* do is tell the managing partner (or any other partner you happen to come across) before you've tackled it with the errant partner. That could easily cause unnecessary bad feeling. If you really are struggling, you could ask the managing partner or another partner for words of wisdom on how to raise the matter – but do not ask them to raise it for you. That's not how strong teams work.

There must be no place to hide for an equity partner who does not deliver on promises made. This does not just apply to action points, but also to behaviours – if you think another member of the top team is not living the values, then you must hold them to account on that.

There may be an exception to all that I have said. If you believe something really serious is happening, maybe something dishonest, or an untruth, it may be wise to discuss this with the managing partner or another senior partner. These things may be better tackled in a different way, outside a top team meeting.

13.11. Succession planning

The top team has one more role – and that is to think about succession planning.

It needs to make sure there is a good supply of people in the firm ready to step up as equity partners. This is important and in everyone's best interests. Senior staff want to see there is a route for them to the very top. Senior partners want to make sure that when they retire there are good people to keep the firm going and continue their good work.

And the top team needs to make sure there are people amongst their number who would be suitable candidates to replace the current managing partner when she steps down.

I had heard so many horror stories, mostly from accountants, about what a terrible job many law firms make of handing over the baton to the next generation. I was determined not to make that mistake. I had been the managing partner for over 30 years, so this was going to be a big change for us.

I suggested we needed a seven-year plan, with a view to me stepping down as managing partner about half way through the plan. Two years to select the new managing partner. Then a two-year handover of the managing partner role (in the first year, the new managing partner shadowed me, and in the second year they took the title and I mentored them). The plan allowed time for us to go backwards and for me to take the role again in the short-term if, for any reason, we didn't get it right, but I'm pleased to say that hasn't been necessary.

It's critical that the top team is always thinking about who the next equity partners will be and making sure that the team includes people who can potentially be the next managing partners.

13.12. When you get it right

When the members of the top team like and trust each other, and when they make decisions in a way where everybody listens, contributes and challenges until there is agreement about a course of action then you will have a business where great decisions are made. Where the top team is totally committed to implementing these decisions and to bringing the rest of the firm on board then you will have strong leadership. This will lead to happy staff, happy clients and a profitable business.

A few great questions

1. Do you already have some rising stars who you have identified as your future equity partners? If not how are you going to change that?

2. What about the next managing partner – are there one or two people in the top team who could take the role right now, in case of an emergency?

3. Are you doing enough to build the top team as a team? Are you investing in away-days and team-building exercises?

4. Do you have good processes for making the big decisions?

5. Are all the partners committed to holding each other to account on promises made?

Rule 14:
Fight for your beliefs!

As leader you must be completely intolerant of 'off-message' behaviour and ready to fight for your organisation's values and beliefs. You need courage, determination, intolerance and sheer bloody-mindedness. If something's not right – that's your fault – that responsibility is yours! It's your intolerance of what's wrong, and your discipline in pursuing what's right, that will make the organisation great. Your focus on pursuing decisions that were made will move the organisation forward.

Getting clarity on why your firm exists and having a motivating vision are very important, but it's the actions you take day in and day out that tell people you believe in your plan and you are going to see it through. The truth is that most of the time we all know what we should be doing – it's *doing* it that's the hard part. You, the leader, must commit to doing the tough stuff!

14.1. Intolerance takes courage

Good decisions are made in a relaxed and calm environment. But those decisions have to be implemented in the day-to-day chaos of the business world. We can all make great plans for getting fitter or slimmer – but sticking with the diets and exercise regimes is much harder! It takes strength, courage and determination to take the necessary actions.

In the boardroom, it's easy to decide that you'll turn away work if you don't have the capacity to do it well. But it's much harder to say 'no' to a client who's on the phone offering you a really interesting piece of work. My experience is that many lawyers just do not believe that we really do want them to turn away profitable work. But if that's the decision you made because you decided that exceeding clients' expectations is important – that this is a value you want to be judged on – then that work must be declined. You must support, recognise and reward the lawyer who does it, and be intolerant of any lawyer who doesn't. There must be consequences for those not following the decision through, starting with a face-to-face conversation. As soon as you start to tackle those who are not complying, word will get out and your job will get easier. If you don't tackle every single instance of non-compliance then that strategy is doomed to failure and you become like every other law firm that does good work most of the time, not the standout firm that does excellent work all the time. The point of differentiation is lost.

As described in Rule 8 the most important place to be intolerant is with recruitment mistakes! It's so hard to find the right people, and even harder to dismiss a great lawyer who's smashing fee targets but whose client feedback isn't amazing. But if exceeding client expectations is high in your values list, then they will have to be dismissed. This is where the leader must lead. It will be a hard job for the line manager who has to deal with the departure, and they must be confident that the leader and all the top team are right behind them. It's not that you're saying goodbye to a bad person, just to someone who happens not to share your values. Your intolerance of this will free them up to be happier somewhere else, while keeping the integrity of your organisation intact. This is a decision to be celebrated.

14.2. Keep your eye on the ball!

You spent a lot of time preparing the business plan – see Rule 5. It's your job to keep everyone focused on it. The business plan is your job description. As leader, you must do everything you possibly can to deliver the promises in that plan. You'll need to use all your skills in inspiring, motivating, encouraging and cajoling to get others to do what they promised to do, so that you can deliver the plan. If others fail to deliver on their promises, you must address that with them and make the consequences clear if they don't put the matter right. Your intolerance will make your organisation great.

I recommend examining the plan at least once a month, when you set your own work agenda for the month. Have it to hand for all your meetings with those you manage, alongside their individual goals. Your performance will be measured by how you deliver the plan.

Think about any new opportunities that present themselves during the year – these can be very exciting. But think carefully – can you make the new opportunity work and still deliver the business plan? If so, great. If that's not possible, is this new opportunity more important than the original plan? If so, this is top team stuff and will necessitate a mid-year rewrite of the plan – so you need to be really sure!

14.3. Fight for your beliefs

An organisational belief is a conviction that is held to be true by everyone in the organisation. Religions are good examples of organisations with strong shared beliefs.

Organisational beliefs are important. They're very much like values and are an important part of your culture. Think carefully about your beliefs to make sure they serve you and your firm. It's so easy to pick up beliefs that don't serve. Beliefs can be changed – often all that's necessary is a careful examination of why you chose to hold that belief in the first place and to make a different choice.

So before you choose to fight for a belief, it's worth examining it to make sure it's worth your effort. But when you're sure your belief is solid, you need to fight for it.

When I first introduced our flexible working policy (work when, where and how you like) there was resistance from some of our managers. They didn't understand how we were going to measure how hard people were working.

I didn't want to reward people for working long hours, but for doing their best work and working smart! I wanted to reward people for meeting their goals in the best way they could. I wanted people to work *fewer* hours, for better results! I wanted to abolish presenteeism. I know all about presenteeism because I used to practise it myself, taking pride in working long hours and – even worse – being *seen* to be doing so (first to arrive, last to leave, even when I knew I wasn't really doing anything useful because I was exhausted).

I knew the new policy was the right thing to do. I was unshakeable. I introduced it in September 2003 and guess what happened – absolutely nothing! The workers still worked and the shirkers still shirked! I remain as unshakeable as ever. There's no point in measuring hours. We all know how to sit at a desk and look as if we're working when in fact we're looking up what's on TV tonight or thinking about what to buy for dinner. What I love about this policy is it helps our best people. It makes it possible for them to arrange their lives to suit themselves and it helps make us a great place to work!

Of course managers still have to manage. Their job is the same as it always was – to notice the shirkers and free up their futures. What we do not want to do is create all sorts of monitoring systems to monitor the shirkers – such systems will just hold back the great people.

It is just as important to know when you're *not* unshakeable. Notice how you feel as you say things. Are you rock solid or could someone persuade you to the other view? Are you dithering? Never fight for a belief you're not sure about. Get sure first, because otherwise your audience will know. Remember that only 7% of communication is in the words we speak;[37] you won't be able to hide it when you're not completely confident about what you're saying. So get clear first.

14.4. Unwelcome organisational beliefs

Sometimes organisational beliefs go astray. This happens when there is a weight of contrary evidence, and this is when the leader has to fight hardest.

I noticed this during the depths of the last recession, when all our teams were finding it hard to hit their financial targets. The collective belief was changing from 'these targets are fair' to 'these targets are impossible to attain so there's no point in even trying'. This is dangerous territory. There's no doubt targets are easier to attain in good times, but even in bad times the belief still has to be that the target is fair, with the understanding that a bit of a harder fight might be needed to get there. If targets are not being attained, the leader still has to be intolerant. Just allowing people not to meet the targets is never going to be the right way forward. It will damage the belief that the targets are fair and it will damage the self-esteem of those failing to achieve their goals.

Again, there may be difficult decisions to make in such situations. If the amount of available work is reduced – like in a property recession – then you can either make some people redundant or put more pressure on everyone to go out and improve your market share (which, if there's a shortage of work, there is time to do!). To recognise the plan, you may give a short-term reduction in targets for fees delivered, but increase targets for work brought in.

Personally, I believe it's so hard to find great people that making good people redundant has to be the absolute last resort. But whatever you decide, fight for the belief!

There was a time when we suffered from an unwelcome organisational belief that it's very hard for residential property lawyers to delight clients. Stories were told about why it was so hard – local authority searches take so long, the client has a strong emotional attachment to the house they're buying, we don't have time to get to know them... That all changed when we got our recruitment right. A few years later, the residential property lawyers had the highest levels of client service satisfaction in the firm.

More recently, a belief developed that it's difficult for litigators to delight clients and, again, there were stories to support it – litigation is normally something clients don't want; clients are already angry. But I've seen lawyers in all legal areas consistently delighting their clients. We fought hard and turned this belief around.

It's really important that these unwelcome beliefs are nipped in the bud. That's the leader's job – a time to be very intolerant!

14.5. Slippage

If you set a target you expect to be met, mean it! Targets should be attainable. Our lawyers record the time they spend on client matters so that we can work out which work is profitable. We expect 1,380 hours each year on client work for lawyers with no special management responsibilities. I believe that is a reasonable target – it's at the low end of what most firms expect, with some city firms requiring 1,800 or even 2,000[38] hours each year.

But so often I hear, 'My time's good, I'm at 90% of the target!' That's another organisational belief we've had to fight recently. Don't let things slip – if the target isn't fair, reduce it, but if it's fair, then expect 100%!

14.6. Don't ignore – campaign!

Let it be known in your firm that ignoring policies and procedures will not be tolerated, but that it's always acceptable to suggest changing them.

We make policies, procedures and rules for a reason. I don't think anyone just wakes up and thinks 'I know, I'll make up some new rules today!' There's always a problem that the policy was designed to solve. But it's hard to get it right.

Good law firms are expected to comply with many quality standards, each with its own rules and regulations. During my time as managing partner, the amount of external red tape that we've been required to comply with has multiplied many times over and it's still growing. I spent most of the 1990s writing our office manual. We were very proud when we were amongst the first wave of firms to be awarded a Legal Aid Franchise in 1994 – our first quality mark. But I did go over the top and ended up spending most of the 2000s trying to simplify our procedures!

The rules we have must be complied with, but we really try hard not to have unnecessary ones. I welcome the questioning of the rules. I can always explain the problem the rule was designed to solve, and I'm delighted if someone makes a simpler suggestion to solve that problem. We change rules all the time.

Like most other firms, we now have professional compliance managers. But in my view, they're not there to chase lawyers who don't take their compliance obligations seriously. Anyone who ignores the rules is not a person we can afford to have in our firm. Compliance managers are there to support the right people, not to manage those who don't buy into the need for discipline in the way they do their work.

Always remember that the rules are there to support your best people – to give your EAGLES a solid infrastructure from which to fly. Have as few rules as possible – but then enforce those you do have with an iron will. And never forget the higher someone is in the organisation, the more important it is for them to lead by example. You cannot make exceptions for 'difficult' partners!

14.7. You want to be respected – not liked

Your job as leader is to create a culture where great people can flourish. Where entrepreneurial endeavour is welcomed and recognised. You're there to support your best people. The best way to do that is to be intolerant of anyone or anything that threatens your culture.

When you get this right, you'll attract more of the best people, who will need less management and support. You will not be wasting your time fighting for beliefs or managing disciplinary processes. You will be respected as an intolerant leader – fighting for your culture so that good people can thrive.

A few great questions

1. Do you have any unwelcome beliefs creeping into your organisation?

2. Do you spend enough time talking to your people so that you'd know?

3. Where are you not being intolerant? How is that damaging your business?

4. Do you have any procedures you could scrap?

5. Is it understood in your organisation that campaigning to change rules is encouraged – if you have a better idea?

Rule 15:
Decisions – make them early and make them stick!

As leader, making good decisions is critical and you'll be making many of them every working day.

The thing about decisions is that you will never know what would have happened had you made a different decision. You will never know if you made the best decision – so just get on with it and do the best you can with the information available. Remember that doing nothing is a decision too. A good leader makes timely decisions with a sensible amount of research and consultation and then moves on to the next thing!

To make the best decisions, you need to be able to think logically – so never, ever make decisions in the heat of the moment, when you're not in your human brain! If you're angry, this is the time to take a walk, not to make any decisions.

15.1. Identify when a decision needs to be made

My main regret around decisions is how long I delayed in making some of the really big ones. We dithered for a long time before deciding to cease doing criminal work. It's scary to turn off an income stream. Yet when the decision was eventually made, we never looked back.

Perhaps the biggest decision I ever made was to split the firm. I spent years thinking about the tensions within the firm and whether it would thrive better as two separate organisations before I eventually did it. It was an enormous decision and I'm now sure it was the right one. It just would have been even better made five years earlier!

Decisions that don't get made keep returning like a bad smell. Look out for things that crop up time and time again on an agenda – they're asking for a decision or a different decision to be made.

15.2. Beware of procrastination

It's easy to put off making a decision where the actions that will be involved in the implementation are likely to be unpleasant. Having an honest conversation with a problem employee is not fun, so we put off making the decision to have that conversation. But leaders must be strong and put long-term gain ahead of short-term pain!

Decisions that we put off eat into our energy, making us feel drained and giving us a feeling of inadequacy and self-doubt. Tackling the decision head-on and getting straight on with implementation make us feel good – we can sense the forward progress. Lovely brain chemicals are released and we feel energised and ready for the next thing.

You need to develop strategies to ensure difficult decisions get made and actioned. I learnt this a long time ago when I realised that I hated making difficult phone calls and so I put them off. I created a little routine that started with some nice things – leave desk, make coffee, light cigarette, stand up, pick up phone and dial the number. (It's more than 25 years since anyone smoked in our office – now I just congratulate myself on being a non-smoker! But I still follow the routine – I even think about not lighting a cigarette before a difficult phone call!) With each difficult decision, I put a time in my diary for making it. If other people are involved, I make sure it's put on an agenda. I resolve that a decision will be made at that time.

15.3. Be clear who has authority

One of the reasons a decision fails to get made is that no one is clear whose responsibility it is to make it. Often in a partnership, every partner feels they have the right to be involved in every decision – that is one way to run the organisation, but it's not an efficient way. For an organisation to run effectively, some decisions need to be delegated.

It's not difficult to get clarity on who has authority to make decisions, but it does take time.

Decisions can be put into three categories:

- Those that must be made by a group of people, e.g. the top team

- Those that can be delegated, but where a bigger group needs to be informed before a final decision is made

- Those that need no consultation or prior information.

For example, most partnerships will require that the admission or expulsion of a partner will be agreed at a full partners' meeting. This is not a decision that is delegated anywhere and the right for all partners to be involved is normally reserved in the partnership deed.

If there's a top team which does not include all the partners, then most other decisions will be delegated to it, including all financial and strategic decisions. But there may be some issues where the management team is asked to inform the full partnership before making a final decision, such as opening a new office, starting a new area of work or a huge IT spend – if any partners do not agree then the matter can be elevated to a full partners' meeting.

The top team will delegate most day-to-day decisions to a managing partner – but again, there may be a number of matters where the managing partner is asked to inform others before a final decision is made. For example, the managing partner may have full rights to authorise recruitment, but perhaps needs to inform the top team before bringing someone on board at the most senior level.

The managing partner may, in turn, delegate decisions to e.g. a compliance manager or to legal department heads. The same principles apply.

So the first key to success is investing the time in agreeing who has the authority and responsibility to make decisions. If you don't get it right, unnecessary disputes can arise.

The second key is to make sure that everyone understands who has the authority, and agrees to support decisions properly made in line with that delegated authority – especially those who disagree with the decision. That is not to say decisions cannot be questioned in the appropriate meeting – any decision can always be reversed and all partners always have the right to ask why a decision was made – but outside the appropriate meeting full support must be demanded.

It's not easy to get this right! Even where you think authority is clear, it can sometimes go wrong. For me, this was most famously around what has now become known as 'cardigan-gate'. The office was a mess. People had stuff everywhere – on, under and around their desks and chairs. The office was becoming dirty because the cleaner couldn't get past the mess to clean. I instigated a clean-up campaign, and staff were asked to move coats and cardigans from the backs of their chairs to the cloakroom.

There was outcry!

As managing partner, I was very sure that the responsibility of keeping the office clean and tidy was delegated to me. It never occurred to me how strongly people would feel about keeping their coats with them rather than in the cloakroom! In the end I decided this was not a battle worth fighting and I gave in.

You need clarity about these things. My experience is that partners are very happy to delegate big decisions like spending hundreds of thousands of pounds on a new IT system, but want to be involved in every tiny thing that affects their day-to-day life.

The lot of the managing partner is a tough one!

15.4. How will you make the decision?

When you're responsible for making a decision, it's wise to think about how the decision will be made.

The smallest decisions that affect no one adversely can often simply be decided without consulting anyone else. Sometimes, an email saying 'This is what I am going to decide, unless anyone has a better idea?' is helpful.

Where a lot of people will be affected, consultation may be appropriate. However when you do consult make sure it is clear that this is consultation – not a delegation of the right to make the decision. I often say 'this is not a democracy' because it is not! We value the opinions of all our staff but at the end of the day it is the partners – or those they have delegated to – who are responsible for making good decisions.

15.5. Use a clear process

For the big decisions always start by agreeing the process. I've worked with several different decision-making models – I now use my own PROCEED model,[39] which works for making decisions in a team or on my own:

1. **PROBLEM**

   What is the problem? What are we trying to achieve? State it factually in as much detail as possible – but without presupposing any solution.

2. **RELEVANT SURROUNDING FACTORS**

   What do we need to consider when arriving at a decision?

   a. Who might be affected by this decision? Consider all stakeholders, staff, clients, suppliers, funders, lenders, community – everyone!

   b. Which of our values do we need to take into account in making this decision?

c. Is any part of our strategy or business plan relevant?

d. Are long- and short-term priorities different? Which is more important here?

e. What skills do we have, or lack, that may be relevant to this decision?

f. What resources do we have, or lack, that may be relevant?

g. Are we clear on any relevant law or red tape?

h. Have we made similar decisions in the past – what can we learn from them?

i. Do we know anything about similar decisions our competitors have made?

j. Do we need to do any research before we continue?

k. Anything else?

If more research is needed, pause here whilst that's done and fix a time to continue the process.

3. OPTIONS

What are our options? What else might work that we've never thought of before? This is a brainstorm to encourage new and innovative thinking. Find as many possibilities as you can with no judgement about their viability at this stage. Don't forget to include doing nothing.

4. CONSULT

Now we have a list of options, is there anyone else we want to bring into this process? Should we consult any of those stakeholders who may be affected? Are there any experts we could consult? Would consulting bring any value to the decision? Might it help with buy-in later?

5. EVALUATION CRITERIA

What are the most important criteria going to be in making the decision? Which stakeholders are most important? Which of our values are most important for this decision? How will we decide if we don't all agree? Are we going to continue to debate until the 'feeling of the meeting' emerges or will we defer to a majority view, or follow the view of those most closely affected?

6. EVALUATE THE OPTIONS

Now consider the options. Can we rule any of them out? What are the pros and cons of each option for the most important stakeholders? Which options fit best with our values? Can we combine any of the options?

7. DECIDE A COURSE OF ACTION

Now it's time to create a course of action: decide what will be done, who will do it, what we need to communicate and to whom, and the time frame for implementing the decision.

15.6. Making decisions stick

A decision is useless until it is communicated and implemented. The worst decisions are those that are made but not implemented – when a decision is made but then everyone leaves the room and no one does anything about it! That is just a waste of time and energy and if it happens often it will make people feel meetings are a waste of time. This is why the final step in the PROCEED process is so important. Make sure the decision is recorded and it's agreed who's going to do what – and fix a date for reporting back that the decision has been implemented. An email to those involved, confirming the decision, the action and the time scale, usually suffices.

15.7. Never be afraid of the U-turn

Accept that sometimes you may get it wrong. A decision that somehow refuses to be implemented or that keeps returning to the agenda may be trying to tell you that you got it wrong – or perhaps that there is something more fundamentally broken in the organisation. Put it back on the agenda and apply PROCEED again – particularly noting what didn't work last time and reflecting on what you may not have thought about that you need to consider this time.

15.8. Get a reputation for making decisions

When you create an organisational culture where it is understood that problems are tackled and decisions are made and implemented, you will be a long way along the journey to success. The leader must lead by example – and help and coach others within the organisation to make good decisions.

The consequences are an organisation that's constantly changing and moving forward. An organisation where people know that difficult problems are tackled and that there is constant change for the better.

This is motivating to the very best people – and keeping them happy and motivated is critical for organisational success!

A few great questions

1. Where are you failing to make decisions?

2. Which decisions have you made but failed to implement?

3. Do you have any issues that keep getting back onto the agenda?

4. Before making a big decision, do you have a clear process for how the decision will be made?

5. Are you clear about who has authority to make which decisions?

6. Is there one decision you've been procrastinating about that you could apply the PROCEED model to now?

Rule 16:
Lead on innovation and change

For any business to remain competitive, constant change and innovation are essential. Often the need for change will be as a result of external factors, such as some new legislation. Sometimes a change will be necessary to boost performance, for example where financial results are falling. And sometimes change is not necessary but is rather a desire to innovate – to do something different because you perceive it will give you competitive advantage.

The leader, with the top team, has to decide when change is necessary and plan a route to success.

It's a tricky path to tread: you must balance the need to embed what's going well with the temptation to innovate for further improvement. You need to push forward, but not so fast that people get scared. You want to take up new technology to keep up with the competition but sometimes it may be better to wait a while and let others sort out the bugs!

16.1. Understanding change

When we talk about change, we're most often talking about changing the behaviours of individuals.

Any human behaviour is the result of one of two things:

- A conscious decision made in our human brain (the prefrontal cortex), or

- An unconscious habit – actions we do automatically because they're stored in our memory (in the basal ganglia). We are wired to prefer to keep doing the same things we have always done because those strategies have kept us safe so far.

16.2. Threat as a motivator for change

When we perceive a threat, change will be easier. Our brains are concerned about threat – they want to keep us safe! So where there's a clear threat from failing to change, it's much easier to change our behaviours.

When the government introduced anti-money-laundering legislation, we all had to start doing identity checks on our clients. This was a nuisance – we'd been used to taking instructions over the phone and getting on with the legal work. We had to adapt our client acceptance procedures. No one found this fun. But it was easy to see the consequences of failure to take the action – at worst, jail! The threat was obvious, and lawyers soon learnt to make the necessary changes in routine procedures.

16.3. Inventions that make life easier

New inventions bring changes. When I started work, we used typewriters and carbon paper. The engrossing of a lease and counterpart meant someone had to type the same document twice! The memory typewriter and then the word processor made this unnecessary. There was no problem embracing that change – it made everyone's lives easier.

The invention of fax revolutionised written communication where we previously only had post. Faxes have now been replaced by emails. Again, for most of us, these were very easy changes to embrace, because compared to post and fax, email saves time and money, and has the huge advantage of being desk-to-desk – from the sender to the recipient – instantly.

Our flexible working policy was considered very innovative when I introduced it in 2003. I saw this as a big competitive advantage. I thought staff would like it because it would help them to run their personal lives, and I thought clients would like it because staff would find it easier to offer them more flexible appointment times. I was right. Given that it's critical for us to attract and retain the best staff and the best clients, this innovation has given us a competitive advantage. It was relatively easy to implement because no one was required to make changes – they were just given the option to work more flexibly, should they wish to.

Sometimes, though, innovation will bring resistance particularly where there is no threat and no immediate upside to those who will need to change their behaviour. In Bolt Burdon Kemp, where we're already highly specialised (only doing serious personal injury cases), we decided we'd have a competitive advantage in attracting clients if our lawyers narrowed their specialisms even further – we asked people to choose to specialise in particular types of injury, e.g. child brain injury cases. We felt this was the best way to compete in the market for clients – we know clients like specialists. But for solicitors early in their careers, this is not so attractive – junior solicitors want to gain experience in as many areas as possible. Despite this, we decided that in this case pleasing clients was still the most important thing in the interests of the firm. We worked on other initiatives to get our junior solicitors the broader experience they desire.

16.4. Find ways to get innovative ideas!

The hardest thing about innovation is getting the good ideas. We're such creatures of habit that we rarely notice places where changes can be made.

Innovation can be made in huge ways, like a big reorganisation so we can serve clients better or a huge investment in some specially commissioned computer software. Decisions about this level of innovation are more likely to come from some time away from the office in a creative environment – a top team away-day – perhaps with a visioning exercise.

But small innovations can be made all the time
do this. Find ways to encourage people to think
day tasks can be made easier, and reward the g

16.5. We've always done it like that!

I love asking 'Why do you do it like that?' or 'Have you thought if there's a better way?' Woe betide anyone who replies 'We've always done it like that' – that is never a good reason to keep doing it that way in my book!

I've always been an advocate of time recording and I've always been really clear about why it's important. It's not for checking how long anyone's working, and it's not to decide what to charge a client. It has one purpose only, and that is to help us determine the cost of doing work so that we can figure out what's profitable and what's not.

Many years ago, I was thinking about this in relation to residential property transactions. Time recording is time consuming. I realised that we had ten years' worth of information about residential property transactions and not once had we made any decisions based on that information. The cost of residential property transactions can be measured in a different way. We work in teams of two – a solicitor and a paralegal. We know the salaries and other overheads for these two people. We know how many transactions a month they can deal with and still work sensible hours. The fee is fixed mostly by market forces – we know where we want to sit in the market and we know what sort of fee we want to charge for our service. We need to get more and more efficient, and that means constant innovation and change in how we deal with transactions. But we don't need time-recording information to let us know whether we're achieving that – we can simply count the number of transactions. The day I realised

..is was the day we ceased time recording for residential property teams. The effort was just not justifying the information.

16.6. Don't attempt too much

If there's one big lesson I've learnt about change, it's not to try to do too much at once! Many people find change hard, especially if they're not very enthusiastic about the reason for it.

So before you embark on any change, think about how much effort it will need. Sometimes the new way will be so much easier that it'll require very little effort and all you'll need to do is inform everyone! Other things will need sustained effort. You need to decide if the effort is worth the perceived result and if that change is your priority right now.

If you decide a big change is indeed the most important thing right now, then plan the path to it. Start by getting people on board, and make sure you have the time and energy to make it work.

16.7. 4MAT – how to get everyone on board with change

When the decision has been made to implement a change, I recommend you follow the 4MAT system (developed by Dr Bernice McCarthy[40]) to communicate it to all those who will be affected. I believe this is the most effective way of communicating to a group of people who have a variety of preferred learning styles and ways of taking in information.

4MAT = Why, What, How and What if?

1. First, explain WHY the change is important – those who need a reason to change will disengage if you don't do this

first. Explain carefully the threat you're trying to avoid or the opportunity you're trying to exploit. So, for example, if you have fixed a goal for your organisation to improve realisation ratio (a measure of hourly rate achieved) then explain why this is necessary – to make the business more successful, to ensure there is enough profit for future investment, to allow pay rises, etc.

2. Second, describe WHAT the change is – give facts and information. Some people need a lot of factual information to be convinced, so if there's research to support your change, be ready with it. If you're trying to improve realisation ratio, bring to the table benchmarking information that shows that other similar firms with higher realisation ratios are doing better than you. Demonstrate with a simple dynamic spreadsheet how even a small increase in realisation ratio will make a big improvement in the bottom line.

3. Then HOW – what exactly will individuals need to do? This is important to those who learn by doing – they'll want to try it out, even if just by mental rehearsal. So to improve realisation ratio, what are the actual behaviours that need to change? Perhaps you need to stop taking on work that isn't profitable, so state specifically what that means for your lawyers when talking to clients; rehearse the conversation they are going to have when they tell the client that we don't do that work any more (or perhaps that we will do it but only at an increased fee) but we can recommend another law firm who can do the same type of work to a good standard at a lower fee.

4. Finally, WHAT IF – describe what will happen if you are successful – and what will happen if you fail to make the change. Focus particularly on how the change will affect the people who are going to make it. If you improve realisation ratios, not only will the firm be more successful, but individuals will be able to work fewer hours for the same billed fees!

16.8. Speed of change

It's very important to be clear on how quickly you expect the change to happen.

Remember, change is the result of a decision made in the part of our human brain (the prefrontal cortex) where we do our logical thinking and decision making. Our human brain is only online when we feel safe. If you want people to implement the change, do everything you can to make them feel safe.

Even if we understand the reason for a change, we can feel threatened when we think the change is happening too quickly or too slowly. A solution that is too fast for one person may be too slow for another.

Where there's a choice on speed of implementation, this needs careful thought. Is it possible for people to implement the change at different rates? Can you get a few champions going with it first, who'll then encourage others to join in?

This was possible when we introduced paperless working. There were lots of reasons why we thought it was important: the ability to work anywhere in the world if all documents were stored electronically; the ability for clients to access their matters over the internet; saving trees; reducing paper storage costs. Some of these reasons were not so compelling for some of our lawyers – especially those who chose to do all their work in the office. But there was no rush. We started by making sure that everything was available electronically (scanning incoming post onto files; making electronic filing of all documents compulsory). When we were sure our electronic files were complete, we made paper optional. Those who still wanted to maintain paper files could do so, but it was not necessary. We encouraged people to start throwing paper away and we stopped storing paper files at the end of the matter (we now just destroy them). Some people still keep some paper, but the amount is reducing. We can all access all documents from anywhere in the world, and an unexpected bonus is we've gained huge areas of floor space as the amount of file storage has reduced. I have a little personal celebration every time I see a file storage cabinet waiting to be taken away!

But of course, such a leisurely approach is not always possible, and this is where strong leadership is necessary.

We got it right when we had to implement the Jackson reforms to legal costs. Lord Jackson was appointed to review the costs of civil litigation to promote access to justice at proportionate costs. We knew that from 1 April 2013 there were going to be huge changes to the way conditional fee agreements would work (no win no fee). The new rules would be less attractive to most clients. At the end of 2012, we were still uncertain how exactly it was going to work; the detailed rules were still not published. These were huge changes. We needed to train all our staff and make sure that all clients who would be better off under the old regime got their documents in order in time. We put in place a detailed plan starting in January 2013. We booked out time for compulsory training – even before we knew what the rules would be! We made lists of current and potential clients who may need us to prepare urgent documents for them. We made sure that any potential clients were informed of the changes and the advantages of moving swiftly. Everyone worked very long hours to make sure it was all sorted before the end of March. It wasn't panic – it was the opposite, actually – but it's easy to see how both staff and clients felt under threat by the whole situation. It was an intense time.

Eventually, 1 April 2013 arrived. It hadn't been easy for our people – many of them had been under enormous pressure – but they'd been amazing. All our clients had their documents prepared and signed and the job was done. We were all exhausted but very pleased with our work. For the next few months, we basked in glory as our staff came back from networking events telling us how disorganised some other firms were! Staff in some of these firms were telling our people that they felt they'd let their clients down and were worried about negligence claims.

Our lawyers had been stressed in implementing the changes – however the stress of working for a firm who had not got organised was clearly worse. One we got right! We did the best for our clients and, in the long run, the best for our people, too.

16.9. Making change permanent

The key to making change permanent is to create habits.

Change involves making a conscious decision in our human brain to do things differently, and then applying willpower (more conscious decisions) to keep doing that thing repeatedly. If we do it often enough, and we have enough reason to want to keep doing it, it's possible to embed the action until it becomes a habit, which we will then do unconsciously. That's when you get permanent change. But if we lose motivation too soon, before the new habit has formed, we'll slip back into old habits!

We don't need to think about cleaning our teeth in the morning – it's a habit. We no longer need to think to remember to ask our clients to bring identification documents with them when they come to see us so as to comply with anti-money-laundering legislation – that has also become a habit.

It's easier to create new habits when the change is small. So if the intention is to make a huge increase in realisation ratio, don't attempt to do all the necessary actions at the same time. Start with one small change – perhaps identify work that has the lowest realisation ratio and cease doing that.

Remember that what you measure is what you get, so create measures that will support the change. Identify one change that can be made and focus on this until it's embedded in the firm.

Recognise those who make good choices – celebrate the lawyer who takes action on the decision, or the person or team who's made the biggest improvement. Ask them to speak at meetings about how they managed the process, how they decided to turn a client away and how they did it in a caring way, by referring the client to another excellent firm.

Equally, notice those who aren't making the desired changes. Work out with them in private how they're going to make the change, and gain their commitment to it. Be clear about the consequences if the changes are not made. Give them time – but not too much! Remember, as leader, you must be intolerant (see Rule 14), because if you're not, the rest of the firm will be let down.

It can take a long time to embed a new habit – but it is worth it. If the job is done right the habit becomes embedded in the culture – it's just how we do stuff around here and any other behaviour will never be an option.

16.10. Never stop!

Change and innovation are not occasional things. If your organisation is to remain competitive, change must be happening all the time. The perfect balance is struck when you have constant movement forward at a speed everyone can cope with.

Celebrate change. Encourage everyone to suggest changes. Create a culture of constant improvement.

A few great questions

1. How many changes are you trying to make in your organisation right now? Could it be too few or too many?

2. When was the last time you suggested a tiny change in procedure that would make life easier for someone?

3. What do you think is the invention that will most affect your organisation over the next ten years?

4. Where changes have been made by most people, are you tackling the few that are left behind? Do you have a plan to deal with that reluctant senior partner?

5. Are you creating environments where change and innovation can be explored?

Rule 17:
Do sweat the small stuff!

Never forget that everything you say and do says something about your organisation. You want to be giving a clear and consistent message in every action you take. Do not underestimate the power of the message of how you do the small stuff!

17.1. Why it matters

Recently, I was travelling on an early morning low-cost flight from Gatwick – the plane's first flight of the day. As soon as the seatbelt sign went off, I lowered my tray table and found a coffee cup stain on it. My first thought was, *Heck – if they couldn't do a better job of cleaning the plane, did they manage to service the engines properly?* The next thing I did was look around the plane for further evidence of neglect to support my theory. I noticed a number of small defects that I had not previously been aware of: a snag on the seat cover; a damaged pocket on the back of the seat in front of me; a stain on the carpet. I was now sure the servicing of the engines was likely to be of the same standard.

I go to a brilliant eye surgeon in Harley Street. Well, I say that, but I don't really know how good he is because I'm not qualified to judge the quality of eye surgery. But what I do know is that the premises are spotless, and the coffee is excellent. There's a lot of state-of-the-art equipment and I have endless scans. He takes time when I'm with him. It feels like he cares about my eyes. I sometimes spot celebrities in the waiting room! All these things make me assume he is brilliant.

We make judgements like this all the time. If clients are unable to judge the big stuff (like the quality of legal advice) they'll judge the things they feel able to judge, and assume the same applies to everything. We can't help but do this. It's the way our brains work – we seek patterns everywhere.

17.2. Our brain is a pattern recognition machine

We take in 11 million bits of information every second.[41] This is more information than our brains can process, so we create our own filters, determined by our own values, beliefs and experiences of the world, to make the information more manageable. We each have filters that delete, distort and generalise information to help us store just what we need in the most effective way.[42]

We'll delete information that's not important for us, like what we had for lunch last Tuesday. We often distort information – sometimes we don't take in what people say accurately because we think we already know what they are going to say. We didn't really listen – we just assumed they said what we thought they would say. And we'll generalise – so one coffee stain on a tray table tells me the engine has not been serviced properly.

What's dangerous about this is that once we've made a generalisation, our brain will seek evidence to support it and may delete any evidence that does not! That's why our deep-rooted beliefs may be difficult to shift, because over the years we've gathered a lot of evidence to support them. We look for patterns all the time.[43]

Managing the patterns regarding our business in the minds of others is our 'brand management'. To do this we need to get clarity about the values of our organisation that we want to communicate to others, and then make sure that everything we do sings out these values. In a law firm, the most important groups to communicate our values to are our staff and our clients, but we must also communicate to everyone who comes into contact with our organisation in any way.

Getting this right is not difficult. But it needs thought and, above all, consistency!

17.3. Start with first impressions

If we want to communicate our values of quality and service to our clients and visitors, first impressions are paramount. These first impressions will be the ones that start the process of pattern recognition. I've often said that the most important person in an organisation is the receptionist. The person a client speaks to first, whether in person or on the phone, will create their first judgement about the organisation – the judgement from which all patterns will be created.

For visitors, the whole reception experience is critical. I know our wonderful reception team hold their breath every time I walk into the office. Almost every time I pass through reception, I find something that's not right. I may point out that something needs tidying up or that the flowers are not looking very fresh. Sometimes the temperature's not right, or the jukebox is too loud, or not loud enough. I'm aware this must be very annoying, but I passionately believe that all these things add up to who we are as a firm. One of our values is *excellence in everything we do* – that has to include our cleaning and the quality of our flowers! Those flowers say, 'Welcome, our firm is fresh and bright and we care about making this a lovely place to be'. So I'm afraid my feedback to our reception team is not going to stop anytime soon – every little thing they do matters!

17.4. People

When I was at school, we had to line up every morning and have our shoes and fingernails checked! Sometimes I wish we could do that with our staff at work! Clients will make judgements about your values by the way your people look and behave. This is why airlines spend so much time and money on staff grooming and dress!

It can be hard to address personal issues with staff, but don't shy away from it. Even telling someone they don't smell good can be done with compassion. It's genuinely an act of kindness. If they fail to address it, their whole career could stagnate. Offer training on 'personal brand'. This is especially important for younger people who have often not been told what older clients may expect. Teach them – it is important for their careers. Their casual attitude is not intended to be disrespectful, it is just how they behave with their peers.

As an organisation we need to make sure that our people are shining examples of our own brand values.

17.5. Relationships

We want to offer outstanding service to clients who are prepared to pay a premium for that and we believe that developing long-term relationships with our clients is important if we are to give them the very best service.

If we truly value long-term relationships and paying a premium for service then I believe we should apply these same values to those who supply us. A few years ago, our support team manager told me that he was changing our stationery supplier because he'd found a cheaper company. He was surprised when I questioned this decision, but I knew that our current supplier had gone to considerable effort to supply a few unusual items over the years, and had even made a special delivery to supply some badges we needed urgently for an evening event. When I asked if the new supplier would give us this level of service, I was informed that no, there would just be one weekly delivery. I said no – I would rather pay a little more for a supplier who had proved that they valued our relationship and who had been prepared to provide exceptional service when we needed it.

17.6. Where do you pitch yourself?

When considering brand values, I find it helpful to think about other industries that everyone knows well. Do you want to be perceived like easyJet or British Airways or are you a luxurious private jet? What service are you offering – expertise, experience or efficiency? An efficiency service is better suited to easyJet brand values. An experience service is more in line with British Airways Club Class, in which case the reception had better feel like the Club Class Lounge, and if you are truly offering expertise then nothing should be too much trouble for your clients – think the Concorde Lounge!

It's vital that everything you do is consistent with your brand values. Recently, one of our solicitors asked if she could host an event in our reception for a 'young professionals' networking group she was planning. 'Of course!' I replied. I love it when people want to host events in our office. It's a great way of bringing people in to see our lovely building and to develop relationships that may lead to new business. She suggested that we could reduce the cost if we bought canapés from a local supermarket, and mentioned a budget figure to me. She looked dismayed when I said 'No way!' I laughed and instructed her that if she were to host this event, the people attending must leave saying, *'Wow, that was an amazing event. What a lovely law firm.'* If we were to serve canapés, they must be wonderful. So I told her to put a zero on the end of her budget figure. For me, there's no point hosting an event unless it tells everyone who attends who we are and what we stand for!

Marketing professionals understand this well when it comes to literature – the quality of the notepaper, the feel of the brochure, the communication in the images. We think about our brochures very carefully – but if someone comes into our office and looks at our wonderful literature only to be served a lousy cup of coffee the spell would be broken and all our efforts would have gone to waste!

It is critical to make sure the values run through every tiny thing. You have to sweat the small stuff!

17.7. Proactive management

It's the little things that can be used to communicate values that are harder to express, the things that are not to do with our legal work. One of our values is *'have fun'*. We can communicate this to our clients easily by our jukebox and football table in reception. Our branded products have included flip books with a fun message and stress balls which we sometimes juggle with for our website portraits!

Recently, we were given a great opportunity to demonstrate our *have fun* value to our competitors. RollOnFriday is a popular industry blog about law firm news (much of it tongue-in-cheek). They've regularly made a joke of the pink chair photos on the Bolt Burdon website. So last time, we joined in the humour and sent them a photo of one of our pink chairs with a sign on it saying, 'We ♥ RollOnFriday'. This was published on the site! We'd taken it in good humour and, in return, received free good publicity that completely reflects who we are.

A few great questions

1. What are your organisational values that you want to communicate to your reception visitors?

2. What can you see in your organisation that isn't giving the right message? How can you change that today?

3. Do you personally take responsibility for your organisation's brand? When did you last notice something that was not on message and do something about it?

4. Can you think of any new ways to express your brand values?

5. What about staff training on personal brand – do you offer this to everyone?

RULE 18:
When the shit hits the fan, buy Champagne!

It's in times of crisis that the leader must show the most courage, resolve and leadership. The leader must make sure that the organisation has the best possible chance of coming through the crisis – and that may mean putting on a very brave face!

18.1. The biggest crisis I will ever face

Over the years we've faced our share of difficulties, but the biggest by far was in the early 2000s. At this time, personal injury work accounted for about half of our work, all funded by legal aid. On 31 March 2000, legal aid ceased for most personal injury cases. If we were to continue doing this work we would have to fund it ourselves on a 'no win no fee' basis. We weren't worried about profitability – we knew we were good at this work and that it made good profits. But our cases were mostly serious injuries, and we calculated that without the regular payments from legal aid on average it would take just over two years between doing the work and getting paid for it, even using every trick in the court rule book to get early 'on account' payments from the defendants. The Legal Aid Board had been funding our personal injury work to the tune of about £2m, meaning we'd need to find this amount of working capital from another source if we were to continue trading at our current level.

Our bank really struggled to understand the nature of 'no win no fee' cases, seeing each case individually as uncertain rather than looking at our track record of cases overall and viewing the whole basket of personal injury cases as one risk. We knew our business was sound. I'd worked up a cash flow forecast that we completely believed we could deliver if we could obtain sufficient support from our bank.

After long negotiations and paying for an accountant's report to verify my sums, we were able to negotiate an overdraft facility peaking at £1.6m. This felt pretty scary, to put it mildly. Our whole livelihood was on the line. Our bank was nervous and we were in what our manager liked to call their 'intensive care' department. He constantly told me that he thought we were driving our car faster and faster into a brick wall. I had a weekly appointment at the bank to report on progress.

We knew we could manage our way through the crisis. We also knew there were two critical factors for success: we needed to keep the support of our bank and, even more importantly, the support of our best lawyers. It was our best lawyers who were going to do the work and get the results that would generate the cash.

The bank wanted us to cut back on everything! Reduce staff, reduce every line in the budget and eliminate anything non-essential. Line by line, every single item of expenditure was scrutinised. We didn't want to reduce staff – we had a great team – and forecasts that did reduce staff were even worse than those that didn't. It was impossible to reduce most overheads in the short term, and reducing turnover just meant there was less profit for almost the same overheads. We managed to persuade the bank that the way forward was to maintain the business, perhaps even recruit more staff if that would speed up cases, and do everything we could to push the cases forward to conclusion and payment as fast as possible.

I knew that the most important key to success was to maintain staff morale. If there was anything that was guaranteed to damage that, it was a reduction in all the things that make us a great place to work. I absolutely refused to cut expenses relating to staff – we would give pay rises, we would not cut our training budget and we would maintain our staff welfare programme.

For years we'd had a Christmas 'pros and cons' party (no one quite remembers why we called it this – 'pros' was professionals but what was 'cons' – con artists?). This was an event to which we invited our professional advisors, people who referred clients to us including estate agents, accountants and other solicitors, suppliers, and other friends of the business. We debated hard whether to hold this party in December 2000 but after careful reflection we decided it was essential. We needed to send out a very clear message to our staff and business referrers that it was business as usual at Bolt Burdon. We put on our bravest party face, and we decided to serve Champagne as usual. We had over 100 people attending. That was our way of giving the very clearest message to the world that we were fit and well. For me, the serving of Champagne rather than cheaper fizz at that moment became symbolic of our belief in ourselves. We just made one change – we decided not to invite our bank manager – we just didn't think he would approve.

There followed the hardest two years of my life. We were just two equity partners and at the lowest point on our cash flow forecast we were at the limit of our £1.6m overdraft and negotiating on income tax and VAT payments, and calling in favours from suppliers. I wasn't sleeping. We were tracking the progress of every case. Sometimes the defendants would make an offer to settle a case. Accepting that offer would put immediate cash in our bank. But if accepting that offer was not the right thing for our clients we must not be tempted. We both knew that the minute we felt we hadn't put our clients' best interests first, everything we stood for as lawyers was over. Unacceptable offers were always refused and I made one more phone call to the VAT man asking for yet another extension.

We constantly had to remind ourselves that we had to follow our plan – to do that, we needed to maintain staff morale and keep our best people. So we worked harder than ever to make sure we were a great place to work. We put on a public front of extreme confidence, constantly telling our staff that we were on track with the plan – which we were – and continuing to celebrate every big win.

Eventually, we turned the corner exactly as planned. The cash began to ease, we were able to pay all our suppliers on time, we got the tax and the VAT back on track, and we began to start reducing that overdraft. Make no mistake, we still had several hard years ahead of us in managing the cash – we were only just half-way through the plan – but we had turned the corner.

I learnt a huge amount during that time.

I learnt it was important to acknowledge we had a problem (no one would be fooled by pretending it didn't exist), but also to be supremely confident that we knew how to solve it – this was the truth.

I learnt the importance of keeping the full facts to a very small team; in our case this was the two of us, and our bank manager and advising accountant. I knew others would panic if given the full facts, and my job was to give our plan the very best chance of success. I didn't ever tell any lies though – everyone understood there was pressure!

I learnt a *lot* about cash flow forecasting. It's easy to grow, but short-term shrinking makes cash worse before it gets better! And overheads take time to reduce, if they can be reduced at all.

I learnt that high staff morale was essential – probably the single most important thing – for delivering any plan. We understood that we must look after our people even when we had to borrow money to do so.

And I learnt that the role of the leader is to lead! To make a plan that you believe will work, and then to be supremely confident about your ability to deliver it. You must truthfully and completely believe in its success. If you don't, it's the wrong plan!

A few great questions

1. What is your Champagne – the thing that you do when times are good and that you cling onto when times are bad to demonstrate confidence in your recovery plan?

2. Have you spent time thinking what to communicate in times of crisis and what to keep private?

3. Do you have a small team around you that you can rely on in times of crisis – a great accountant, a good bank manager and perhaps your own personal mentor or coach?

4. Are you really sure you understand how the cash flow works? If not get some training so that you are ready when you need it.

5. Have you generated enough trust in your people that they will stick with you when a crisis hits?

Rule 19:
Be inspirational

Inspire is from Latin – literally 'to breathe into'. Your job as leader is to breathe life into the organisation. You inspire people – that's why they've chosen to follow you. As leader, you'll want to be the best inspiration you can be.

19.1. Choose to be happy, optimistic and energetic

Abraham Lincoln reportedly said, '*Most folks are about as happy as they make their minds up to be.*' I really believe this to be true, and there's a lot of positive psychology to support it.[44] Happiness is a decision. Further, as mentioned in Rule 10 in The Happiness Advantage,[45] Shawn Achor suggests that at work, it's happiness that leads to great results, rather than great results leading to happiness. So being happy will improve organisational success!

One of the things that makes us happy is believing that our lives are meaningful.[46] So always keep in mind that people have chosen to work for your organisation because they believe in what you believe. They believe the organisation does meaningful work. In the day-to-day, it's easy for people to lose sight of the meaning, and to think of daily tasks as 'matters' or 'files' or 'cases' without really reflecting on what success means for clients. But a good leader constantly reminds people why they bother. So bring every success back to your purpose. With every good result for a client, encourage people to think about how their work has improved that client's life – how the compensation you recovered for a client is funding the very best possible care for them – or how your diligence as a conveyancer secured your client the home of their dreams.

If someone feels down because of a poor outcome for a client, make it your job to help them back up and remind them of all the great work the organisation does.

In meetings, have regular 'mission moments' – places on the agenda that offer an opportunity to share how the firm's good work has improved a client's life. Have a slot for successes on all your big agendas.

Think hard about how you can influence happiness in the workplace. Make sure you bound up the stairs in the morning full of energy and ready to go and that you enter meetings in an upbeat mood with a smile and a cheerful 'Good morning!' Others will follow your lead. If you're feeling down, don't let others see it. Of course there will be times when you're down – but that's the time to take a break, and then come back to the office refreshed and renewed.

Take responsibility for the energy of meetings. Start as you mean to go on. I like to start meetings with 'positive beginnings', where everyone shares something positive that has happened in their life recently – there is always something positive in life – maybe you enjoyed the sunshine on the way to work, or you ran a personal best at the parkrun on Saturday. This is not part of the meeting agenda – we are just talking about small things to put everyone in a good mood. There are two good reasons for this: it stimulates the happy brain chemicals serotonin and dopamine, putting us in a positive state for the meeting; and it makes sure everyone gets engaged in the meeting right from the outset, as everyone has to speak.

If during the meeting you feel the energy of a meeting fall, or if you sense a wringing of hands, take responsibility for changing that energy. Suggest a five-minute break so that everyone can walk around the block – walking will raise the energy again.

19.2. Create possibility by being 'at cause'

I believe we each create our own lives. When I talk to groups of people about goals, I invite them to think about how they came to be sitting in the room with me at that moment. I suggest it was as a result of many little decisions they made in their lives: what they studied at school and university, the career they chose, the organisation they chose to work for, the fact that they signed up to be at my talk… it was all their own choice – they created it.

It's the same for leading a business. You have the business *you* created. If you choose to believe this is true, then that's an empowering position. Because if you created it as it is now, you can also choose to make changes and create something different.

You can always choose whether to live 'at cause' or 'at effect'. Being 'at cause' means you believe there is always something you can do to move towards what you want. There is always some action you can take or some new possibility you can explore. You always have options. If you are 'at effect' you are a victim of circumstances. There is always someone to blame for you not getting the results you want. The economy, the weather, the laziness of your staff... You are powerless – you have no choices – all you have is a pile of reasons for not getting what you want.

So choose to believe that you are at cause so that you can determine your future and your organisation's future. After all, your competitors are in the same environment as you! Sometimes external factors will make life tougher, but what makes you special is how you deal with the environment you face. You can make life just the way you want it.

Remember also that when you take action, you'll get one of two things: the result you wanted or some feedback on what doesn't work. If you're truly at cause, you will look at the feedback and think 'OK, that didn't work, but what can I try now to create the result I want?' You will not accept that anything is impossible. All those excuses about the economy, an individual's work ethic or government red tape just slip away. You now see them as constraints to be worked around – just facts, free from any burden of unfairness or injustice. If you're 'at cause', there are always possibilities.

Make time to think about what you've created, including where it's not exactly what you wanted. Make time to get out of the office and get in your imaginary helicopter and see the firm in big overview – look at the wood, not the trees. Spend time thinking about where you are now, and your vision of where you want to be. When you look at the business from high above, you'll be able to see connections that are not visible from deep down in the day-to-day. You'll be able to see which of your initiatives are making progress in the right direction and which are not. You may be able to see where you can start a conversation that will make progress or where silos are developing that you need to break down. In your helicopter, you see your business as a whole, and how it fits with the community and the world around it.

Possibilities will open up. Seek them out and resolve to take action, and keep taking action until you get the results you want.

19.3. Enjoy the vicarious thrill

When you are 'at cause' and living in a world of possibility in which you've taken responsibility for all that is not working, you can also justifiably take credit for everything that is going well! And you should! However, this is normally best done in private – that's why I call it the vicarious thrill. You get your thrill from the success of others which was possible at least in part because of your efforts.

When your organisation has solved a problem or exploited an opportunity as a result of your encouraging or coaching others to take action, all the public praise must go to them. It makes them feel good and inspires more of the same from them, as well as giving a clear message to others that this is a good behaviour.

But privately, you should also be celebrating. This is you doing the job of a leader in the very best way. That vicarious thrill is, in my opinion, the best feeling in the world – the very essence of the joy of leadership. It's what gives meaning to the leader.

Encourage all the leaders in your organisation to 'enjoy the vicarious thrill' and then privately celebrate together!

19.4. Service

Your role as leader is to help others succeed – in other words, to serve. The role of the leader is to serve the organisation and its people. I believe you best serve your organisation when you help your people to grow – when you give them challenges, encourage them to believe they can master those challenges, and coach them to come up with their own solutions to the problems they encounter on the way.

It's the job of front-line lawyers to serve clients. It's the job of the leader to serve those front-line lawyers and others who work in the organisation.

But don't confuse service with caring and compassion. Serving people is not about being nice to them. Of course there will be times when individuals will need your care and compassion. But in the normal working day it's service that's important – doing what you need to do to encourage your people to grow, to tackle jobs they haven't faced before, and to take on new responsibilities. That can take courage – sometimes you may even need to be cruel to be kind!

Service is time consuming. You can't serve everyone all the time. You need to get your priorities right. Your first duty is the most pressing need of the organisation. And the people that you must serve first are the best people in the organisation – those who share the organisation's purpose, values and beliefs and who are most able to help make the firm successful. This is important because these are also the people who are likely to be least demanding – they get it already! They'll need less coaching and less redirection – but neglect them at your peril. It's easy to get completely focused on trying to coach and redirect those who are stepping out of line that you forget about your best players. But be clear – the reason you're spending time with these underperformers is because you must *protect* your best players. As leader it is your responsibility to not let your best people down and to do this you must be intolerant of unsatisfactory performance elsewhere.

19.5. Your leadership style

Develop your own leadership style. Do this consciously. Find the ways that serve your organisation best.

19.5.1. Be a good listener

People want to be heard. As leader, listen to what people have to say. Very often what's most important to them is that they feel their voice has been heard – even if you then have to tell them that you don't agree with them. Listen first to understand, not to respond. To let someone know they've been heard, repeat back to them what they told you. Say something like, 'Just let me check I've understood you. What you'd like is...'. Then, once you're clear, you can go on to say what you think about their view. Maybe you'll think about it, maybe you'll raise it at a meeting, or maybe you're just going to tell them right now that you disagree. They might not be happy with what you say, but they will feel heard, and that's much better than feeling ignored.

19.5.2. Encourage learning

Make sure you've created a learning environment, where training is encouraged, both formally and informally. Reward those who share their learning – their mistakes and what's working well for them. Reward those who say 'I made a mistake – and I'm going to tell you about it so others don't do the same'. Reward those who say 'I don't know – but I'll go and find out'. Reward those who ask for help rather than plough blindly on. Lead the way by constantly learning yourself.

19.5.3. Use a coaching style

I used to be very directive – I'd thought about things carefully and believed it was quicker just to tell people what to do! But this was often not getting the results I wanted and I found myself nagging people to get things done. There is a time for being directive, e.g. when there really is no choice in what to do or how to do it or when it is critical the job is done now – but generally for important issues there is a better way.

I have now discovered that a coaching style works better. Coaching involves talking to people about the need to make changes, encouraging them to explore options and to come up with their own solutions and then supporting them in the implementation. People are much more likely to implement the necessary changes if they make their own decisions on the action to be taken.

Sometimes all it needs is a simple question. Recently I was talking to a solicitor about how she was going to achieve her chargeable hour target. She couldn't decide between staying later each evening or working a solid weekend to catch up – both involved sacrificing time with her son. I asked a simple question 'are those the only options – how many other ways can you think of?' Immediately she came up with more options, shorter lunches, earlier mornings, reading and thinking on the train... and quite quickly she had a plan that didn't sacrifice time with her son at all! Asking good questions is the essence of coaching.

19.5.4. Praise

Make it your business to catch someone doing something right and offer some praise for it. I've been surprised time after time by how much a little recognition from the leader means to people in the organisation – especially the most junior people. See Rule 11.

19.5.5. Lead by example

Leading by example is the only effective way of leading. If you say one thing and do another your trust and respect will be diminished.

When you lead the way you want others to lead you will be an inspiration to the whole organisation. If people respect you, people will copy your way of doing things.

If you choose to be happy and optimistic, others will follow your lead. If you choose to be at cause, others will do the same. If you lead by serving others – listening, learning, coaching and praising – others will want to follow your lead.

A few great questions

1. Are you choosing to be happy? If not, what's stopping you?

2. Do you regularly remind yourself and your people about the business 'why' – how your work makes a positive influence on this world?

3. Could you do more to take responsibility for the energy of meetings?

4. Where are you not at cause? What are your favourite excuses?

5. Hop into your imaginary helicopter right now. What things are going well, and what things are going wrong?

6. Do you enjoy your private celebrations of the vicarious thrill?

7. Are you working on your own leadership style? Do you think you could do more to get the best out of people?

Rule 20:
Do your best work – live your best life!

Managing a law firm is a tough gig! It is constantly demanding and at times can be very stressful. To be able to deal with the demands of the job you need to be on top form – you want to do your best work and to do this you need to be your best self.

I have spent many years honing my philosophy for my best work and my best life:

> *I believe I do my best work – and live my best life (i.e. most meaningful and most successful) when I know*

myself (where I am now, where I want to get to and who I want to be on that journey) and then:

- *I put my own self-care first so that I am healthy, happy and human (Lynne Lynne!)*

- *I make time for my relationships with those I love and care about*

- *I prioritise the work that has the most meaning or is most important to me right now.*

Then I feel happy and free.

20.1. Know who you are

It constantly surprises me how many people have not invested any time in working out who they are and what they want. If you don't know this you won't ever know what will make you feel happy and fulfilled.

You learn where you are now – what your current map of the world looks like – by exploring your current values and beliefs. By looking at your life choices so far and thinking about why you made those choices. By thinking about what it is that you love, what gives your life meaning, what you are passionate about.

You can then think about where you want to go – really plan your life journey so that at the end of it you feel you have lived a good life, a fulfilled life. So that at the end of your life you feel you have made the contribution to the world that you wanted to make.

When you know yourself you know the sort of person you want to be as you go about this journey – what is important to you – kindness, courage, fairness... It will be different for us all. I like to have three 'guiding lights' – three words or phrases that I can hold in my head all the time as I go about my daily life. Mine are:

'*at one*' meaning harmony with the natural world, acceptance of self and others, and living in the present moment; '*tread lightly*' meaning living life with ease, with laughter and with time; and '*best me*' meaning healthy, magical and authentic (having the courage to be the real me).

The more clarity you have about who you are now, where you want to go and who you want to be, the easier it will be to show that to the world – and that is important because as leader you need the trust of those who follow you. Before people can trust you, they need to know you. You won't be able to help others know you if you do not know yourself.

When you do really know who you are it will be easy to be strong and confident and you will feel safe exposing the real you to the outside world.

20.2. Make your own self-care your absolute top priority!

To come to work each day with energy and positivity, you need to be healthy. Without your health you cannot do anything – you can't lead and you can't serve. Your good health is critical to the success of the organisation. To do this demanding job you need to be in good shape – in mind and body. If you are not healthy you may not even be able to come to work at all– so make your health your very top priority!

I have developed my own six SS formula for health and self-care – and each day I think about these six things in my journal and reflect on how I am doing with each of them – where I need to make improvements.

20.2.1. Savour and sip

This one is about nutrition – what I put in my body. Am I eating lots of good fresh food and savouring every mouthful? I know that this is how I choose to eat when I am feeling good. When stressed I know I reach for the carbs – stuff them in – sometimes not even bothering to sit down to eat!

Am I sipping lots and lots of water – and just a little top quality wine? When stressed I know the water gets forgotten and I may drink a few glasses of wine without even noticing! An office culture can be an alcoholic one and I, like many, have a tendency to use alcohol as a release from the pressures of work. Watch carefully for the line between enjoying a drink and needing a drink.

20.2.2. Sweat and stretch

I enjoy exercise! It took me a while to work that out – for many years I thought I hated it, probably a leftover from standing on the freezing hockey pitch at school! I love the feeling of my body moving when I train in the gym. I love being outdoors – sailing, skiing, running, walking my dog on the beach. As I get older I notice my body being less flexible – so now I know I need to include more yoga, Pilates or just having a good stretch!

So why do I so often fail to do it? My excuse is always 'that I don't have time'. This is a very poor excuse – I tell myself that as long as I have time to watch an hour's TV or read a newspaper I have time for exercise. Schedule in time for exercise – and make it sacrosanct. Put it in your diary and fight for that space as if your life depends on it – it does!

20.2.3. Sleep and snooze

Good sleep may be even more important than good nutrition and good exercise. There is increasing research to show how important sleep is and how poorly we function at work if we don't get enough.[47] Apparently all adults need around eight hours every night[48] – I fear most of us rarely achieve that.

So many of us are sleep deprived – the combined pressure of work and family make it very hard not to be. Social events often go on late into the night but we all still set the alarm for an early morning to get the kids to school or get to work on time. You have to find ways to ensure you get regular and sufficient sleep. These days I prioritise my morning time. I love to be up by 5.30am at the latest– so I make late nights rare occurrences and most days I am asleep before 10pm.

20.2.4. Sanctuary and soul

We have to look after our minds as well as our bodies. How we do this will be different for each of us – but I do suggest it needs attention every day.

My most important time each day is the time I spend with my journal. Every morning, at around 10am, I take half an hour on my own for a coffee in the coffee shop. That's my daily time for thought and reflection. I reflect on my life and my work. I record my thoughts in my journal. In the evening I spend time with my journal again – this time reflecting on the things I am grateful for that have happened during the day.

I also love to meditate – but I have to be honest and say that I find it hard to commit to this in the middle of a busy working week. My favourite way to meditate is to set the timer for five minutes on my phone, then just relax, focusing on my breath and letting my thoughts pass by. I give myself the gift of five minutes just to do nothing. At weekends when life is quieter I meditate without the timer – and just stop when I am ready. I know many people love guided meditations – try 'Headspace' – website or app.[49]

Learning is good for your mind. I think we all need to be learning all the time. I always want to be learning something. These days I love to learn more about how our brains work and why we choose to behave the ways we do.

Adventure is important too – where do I want to go, what do I want to see – am I ticking off those things on my bucket list? Yes I am! Holidays are really important for everyone – recreation time, *re-creation*, renewing. Make sure you get some holiday time without emails – give your mind a well-deserved rest! I have trouble with this as I love thinking about work, so I choose activity holidays to keep my mind occupied on different things like sailing, skiing or walking. Try narrow boating – it's amazingly relaxing! Find your own ways to give your mind some time off work.

I also think it is important to look after your spiritual side. This will mean something different to everyone. Those who are committed to a religion will nurture their spirit there. I find it in nature – I'm in awe of the beauty of this world and the good in people. I love to walk in nature and reflect on the magnificence of the trees, the sea, the stars and the wonderful things I see people doing for each other every day.

And finally allow yourself time to just chill... to do nothing... to engage in a bit of rubbish TV or a romantic novel – whatever is your own guilty pleasure!

20.2.5. Surroundings and stuff

I believe the things we surround ourselves with have a huge influence on how we feel.

We all know it feels good when we take time to get a shower and dress in fresh clothes. Invest some time and money in your appearance. Look after your hair, teeth and nails. These things give us a powerful message as to how we value ourselves 'I am worth it'! Think about your clothes – clean and pressed? I like to invest in a beautiful watch and good jewellery – and of course great shoes! These things make me feel good.

I feel good when I am working in a beautiful place – for me that's best if it includes a sea view! We can't always have everything we want but we can always do something to improve our surroundings. Each week I want to do something to make my house just a little bit more beautiful – maybe paint a wall or just throw some junk away.

I beg you to think the same about your place of work – if you provide a beautiful work environment I really think this helps people to work in a more calm and purposeful way.

20.2.6. Saving and spending

Financial health is important – you won't be able to do your best work if you are worrying about money. The trick is to be on top of it – like everything else in life you need a plan!

Warren Buffet advises 'Do not save what is left after spending: instead spend what is left after saving'[50] and I think these are very wise words. Every month make saving a little for your old age or a rainy day important. I have learnt that if a little money for savings is taken from your bank account on the same day as your income comes in you don't even miss it!

I don't spend a lot of time every day thinking about money but I do have a plan and I know when I'm straying from it. I will retire with a healthy pension fund – due to diligence in contributing something to it every single month since 1988!

I know I work better when I have these six things under control. When I'm in good shape in each of these areas I know I arrive at work full of vitality with a spring in my step! That doesn't happen every day but I know that as long as I am paying attention to these things I am aiming for health and happiness.

20.3. Make time for your relationships with those you love and care about

We all have many relationships in our lives that we think are important. If these are to flourish they need care and attention. I believe it is impossible for anyone to do their best work unless they have strong healthy relationships at home. We have all heard the stories of lawyers who work all hours with the inevitable end of burnout and divorce. So make sure you spend enough time with your family. I do regret how little time I spent with my children when they were young. I was working so hard that even when I was with them I was exhausted. In those days I thought the answer to everything was to work harder – I was wrong.

Make time for your friends and your wider community too. These relationships are important in providing you with lots of places where you feel that sense of belonging. That really does make us feel better – and therefore better able to do our best work.

Do not forget your relationships at work. Take time to get to know those you work with and to help them to get to know you. Talk about yourself. Find opportunities to tell people about your background, your childhood, what you love, what you're passionate about and what makes you angry. This is how you will build trust. This has to be real. People will know if you're not being authentic. The human brain is constantly seeking out signs that something's not quite right. This is the job of the amygdala, deep in the mammalian brain. It's constantly searching for signs that something's not quite right and is very good at spotting incongruence in human behaviour. We've all experienced that feeling about someone – 'I don't know…, there's just something about them that doesn't feel right…' – that's your amygdala giving you a clear warning sign.

Don't be afraid to show your vulnerability too when it feels right to do so. You need to be seen to be human – and it's good to show emotions sometimes.

Be brave. Say who you are and what you stand for. Have the courage to do this. It will make you feel amazing.

20.4. Prioritise the work that has the most meaning or is most important to you right now

This is so easy to say and so hard to do!

Our days are filled with urgent demands – the need to pay the gas bill, to get the kids to school, to answer the phone, to reply to that client email that is awaiting attention! It is very hard to find the space to do the work that you really want to do – the work that you know will really make a difference.

For everyone the solution will be different – but if you don't find some time for your most important work then you will live your whole life at the mercy of other people's demands.

My recommendation is that you find what I call a 'magic two hours' every day. Two hours when you make an appointment with yourself to do your most important work. That might be thinking about the business plan, planning a speech, dealing with some important drafting – the things that need peace and quiet and no email or phone interruptions. Just think about it – two hours a day, five days a week, 40 weeks a year is 400 hours of top quality thinking and writing time. Do you think that would help you do a better job?

Finding this time isn't easy. I think the trick is having a routine that works for you – the same two hours every day. I have found the solution in my magic mornings... a pretty unshakeable morning routine. I get up around 5am – drink herbal tea (I really want coffee but that feels like too rude an awakening for my body!) and reflect briefly on my intentions for the day ahead. My magic two hours are 6am to 8am – at my desk with no interruptions except a break after one hour to make my first coffee of the day. 8am to 10.30am is my 'me' time – exercise, shower and dress for work, then time for my journal and a coffee – usually in a coffee shop – it's nice to get out! I'm then ready for my work day to officially start at 11am with two hours work and my 'me' time already under my belt – I feel smug!

20.5. Balance

Make sure you get the balance right between 'me', 'those I love and care about' and 'work'. All are important. Think about what is the right balance for you at this stage of your life. Plan your time to give you this balance. Work may get the biggest time allocation, but you won't be your best at work if you're worrying about your family or if you're burnt out because you've had no chance to rest or relax.

20.6. Ask for help – get a coach!

None of this is easy! I believe in seeking the best help I can find. We don't hesitate to do this in other areas of our lives. I invest in a personal trainer, a financial advisor, a hairdresser, a dentist... the list is endless.

However the best investment I have ever made in myself was to get myself a coach. I have had a few coaches over the years at various times in my business life. But eventually I found the right man for me – Dax Moy.[51]

The purpose of a coach is not to advise on business matters – you have accountants and consultants and all manner of professional advisors for that – the purpose of a coach is, in my view, to help you be your best you – to help you do your very best work.

A good coach will ask good questions, help you explore options and make choices – but will not make the decisions for you. A good coach will support you in the execution of those choices and will challenge or even confront you when you are making excuses – always with your best interests at heart. I've worked with Dax for many years now. He's kept me sane at the worst moments, kept me grounded in the best moments, frequently helped me deal with work stress and overwhelm (sometimes insisting that the best use of our coaching session was to meditate right now!) and, more recently, helped me navigate my route to retirement.

I have become so convinced of the benefits of coaching that I've spent the last few years training to be a coach and I have now made it my new career.

If you are interested in exploring whether a coach might help you to do your best work take the quiz on my website **www.lynneburdon.com/best-test**

20.7. Celebrate your successes!

There isn't a lot of glory in being a good leader. I believe the best leaders engage in quiet dedicated service.

As leader you will mostly ensure that the glory goes to colleagues – you will take your pleasure in what I call 'the vicarious thrill'.

However it is really important to make sure you do recognise your role in the success, even if only to yourself. Have your own private reflection and celebration in the part you played. If other leaders were involved too celebrate privately with them. This is important – remember we all need reward and recognition and sometimes as leader you are going to have to give that to yourself.

However there are moments when you, as the figurehead of the organisation, get to step into the limelight. You will have opportunities to speak to your organisation. You may get to present the business plan or some awards at the Christmas party – both opportunities to bask in all the firm's successes. You may be asked to contribute to conferences or to conduct training on something your organisation does particularly well – to blow your own trumpet. Perhaps you will be asked to receive an award on behalf of the firm.

These are your moments of public recognition, when your happy brain chemicals will be flowing, and when you can take the credit for the success of the organisation.

Be very proud and enjoy these rare moments in the sun!

A few great questions

1. Are you looking after your own health? What small change could you make to improve your physical health?

2. Are you looking after your mental health? Do you do something every day to create a little sanctuary for your mind?

3. Do you have daily time for thinking and planning? Where could you put this in your life?

4. Have you got your work–life balance right? If not what are you going to do about it?

5. Do you invest in your work environment – do you believe this is an investment that will return better work?

6. Do you need more support? Might a coach help?

7. Do you take time to celebrate your successes and to enjoy your rare moments in the sun?

In conclusion

If you have read this far I'm hoping that you see, and agree, that your role as leader is quite simple: to have clarity on what is important; to get the right people on board; to create the conditions for them to thrive – and then to get out of the way and allow them to do that!

You must be clear about your organisation's core purpose (what you are trying to achieve) and your core values (what is most important about how you behave). You need a clear vision of what success looks like.

You must do whatever it takes to make sure that everyone in the organisation shares this ideology – which they will if you have surrounded yourself with people whose own values are in alignment with those of your organisation.

Then it is important that you understand something of how human beings work – what is hardwired within us – so that you can create an organisation where good people can thrive and fulfil their own intrinsic motivation – do their 'best' work rather than their 'most' work. In my organisational jargon – create an environment in which EAGLES can soar...

So often leaders spend their time trying to solve problems or improve performance by looking at the end of the supply chain, i.e., products (Should we start offering a new type of work? Do we need to reduce fees?) and productivity (Do we need to buy new IT? Is our leverage right?), and of course these are valid questions – but they are not the place to start.

The true key to success is at the other end of the chain – if you have happy people who are passionate about what the organisation does they will constantly be making suggestions about how to improve products and productivity – the leader will only need to nod and say 'go for it!'

I encourage you to constantly ask yourself these questions:

- Where in our organisation do we have practices or procedures which are promoting the wrong behaviours, e.g. a bonus scheme that rewards fees collected when we are trying to create an environment where work is passed to the person best placed to serve the client?

- Where in our organisation are we using controls or restrictions to create compliance rather than asking who is not on board with what we are trying to achieve? How can we better design our working environment to be more supportive for our best people – giving them more freedom and trust so that they can do their best work?

- Where in our organisation is there confusion and misunderstanding? Where can we see evidence of that? What can we do to improve our communication to make sure everyone understands what we are trying to achieve and how we need that to be done?

I hope you will pick this book up from time to time when you're facing a leadership issue, to remind you to focus on the fundamentals rather than just looking for the sticking-plaster solution. Revisit the questions at the end of each chapter occasionally: just thinking about them will set your unconscious mind to work on innovative solutions for your own organisation

May I help you further?

Are you interested in receiving my regular reflections and tips on leadership and growing strong teams? Sign up for my blog: **www.lynneburdon.com/blog**

Are you are interested in exploring where you are not doing your best work? Take the quiz on my website: **www.lynneburdon.com/best-test**

If you think coaching might be for you – have a look at how I work one to one: **www.lynneburdon.com/work-with-me/coaching**

If you are seeking someone to work with your top team – or any team – to improve performance have a look at **www.lynneburdon.com/work-with-me/work-with-groups**

If you are interested in attending one of my training sessions or organising bespoke training for your organisation: **www.lynneburdon.com/work-with-me/training**

Do you run events and conferences and seek inspiring speakers? Have a look at my speaking page: **www.lynneburdon.com/talks**

If you would like to work with me in any way please visit my website **www.lynneburdon.com** or contact me on **lynne@lynneburdon.com**

Further reading

There are a few authors who have hugely influenced my thinking. I refer to them whenever I remember this is where my learning came from but I suspect there is much more in my book that is influenced by these authors.

Stephen Mayson – surely the most knowledgeable thought leader on law firms. His book *Making Sense of Law Firms,*[52] now 20 years old, remains my bible whenever I want to go back to first principles of understanding how a law firm works. His second book *Law Firm Strategy*[53] developed my understanding of competitive advantage and ownership.

Simon Sinek – *Start with Why*[54] and *Leaders Eat Last*[55] are must reads for every business person.

Jim Collins – I pick up his books all the time – especially *Built to Last*[56] and *Good to Great.*[57] These books are the results of academic research but are easy to read and contain real gems of business understanding.

Patrick Lencioni – I was only recently introduced to his work. I must now have bought hundreds of copies of his books which I give to our staff because they are so readable – particularly *The Ideal Team Player*[58] and *The Five Dysfunctions of a Team.*[59]

David Maister – especially *Managing the Professional Service Firm*[60] written in 1993 but still a great read and a book I often give to our new managers.

Jay Lorsch and Thomas Tierney – *Aligning the Stars*.[61] A brilliant book that explores the tri-party relationship between clients, professionals and the organisation.

Daniel Pink – his book *Drive*[62] completely changed my understanding of reward systems.

Ruby Wax – *Sane New World*.[63] The book that gave me a humourous and simple understanding of how our brain works.

Shawn Achor – my most recent discovery – *The Happiness Advantage*[64] and *Before Happiness*.[65]

Notes

[1] Jim Collins and Jerry I Porras *Built to Last*, 10th Anniversary Edition (Random House Business Books, London 2005)

[2] Simon Sinek *Start with Why* (Portfolio Penguin, London 2011)

[3] Jim Collins and Jerry I Porras *Built to Last*, 10th Anniversary Edition (Random House Business Books, London 2005) Preface page xiv

[4] Yellow pages – a now almost obsolete telephone directory for businesses. https://en.wikipedia.org/wiki/Yellow_pages

[5] I did make one big mistake with the split – allowing each new firm to keep the Bolt Burdon name. The two firms became known as Bolt Burdon (doing commercial and private client work) and Bolt Burdon Kemp (doing personal injury litigation). This has led to confusion ever since!

[6] Sir David Clementi was commissioned by the government to undertake a review of the legal profession and 'consider what regulatory framework would best promote competition, innovation and the public and consumer interest in an efficient, effective and independent legal sector'. His report was delivered on 15 December 2004 and can be found at http://webarchive. nationalarchives.gov.uk/ and http://www.legal-services-review. org.uk/content/report/index.htm

[7] Jim Collins *Good to Great* (Random House, London 2001)

[8] Michael Porter *Competitive Strategy* (Free Press, New York 1980)

[9] David Maister *Managing the Professional Service Firm* (Simon & Schuster UK Ltd, London 2003)

10 Diane Ackerman "I Sing the Body's Pattern Recognition Machine". *The New York Times*, 15 June 2004 www.nytimes.com/2004/06/15/science/essay-i-sing-the-body-s-pattern-recognition-machine.html

11 Stephen Mayson *Making Sense of Law Firms* (Blackstone Press Limited, London 1997)

12 https://en.wikipedia.org/wiki/Albert_Mehrabian

13 Jim Collins *Good to Great* (Random House, London 2001) Chapter 3 p 42

14 John Ridgeway – see https://en.wikipedia.org/wiki/John_Ridgway_(sailor)

15 A H Maslow (1943). "A Theory of Human Motivation". *Psychological Review*. 50 (4): 370–96. doi:10.1037/h0054346 http://psychclassics.yorku.ca/Maslow/motivation.htm

16 Frederick Herzberg *The Motivation to Work* (Routledge, Abingdon, Oxon 2017)

17 Carnegie Mellon University. "How Stress Influences Disease: Study reveals inflammation as the culprit". *ScienceDaily*, 2 April 2012. www.sciencedaily.com/releases/2012/04/120402162546.htm; Emily Dean MD. "How Stress Makes You Sick and Sad". *Psychology Today*, 27 March 2011. www.psychologytoday.com/us/blog/evolutionary-psychiatry/201103/how-stress-makes-you-sick-and-sad

18 Emma Seppala and Kim Cameron "Proof That Positive Work Cultures are More Productive". *Harvard Business Review*, 1 December 2015. https://hbr.org/2015/12/proof-that-positive-work-cultures-are-more-productive

19 Shawn Achor and Michelle Gielan "Resilience Is About How You Recharge, Not How You Endure". *Harvard Business Review*, 24 June 2016. https://hbr.org/2016/06/resilience-is-about-how-you-recharge-not-how-you-endure

20 https://en.wikipedia.org/wiki/Dunbar%27s_number

21 Tony Hsieh *Delivering Happiness* (Business Plus, New York 2010)

22   Richard M Ryan and Edward L Deci *Self-Determination Theory* (Guilford Press, New York 2017)

23   Frederick Herzberg *The Motivation to Work* (Routledge, Abingdon, Oxon 2017)

24   Daniel Pink *Drive* (Canongate Books, Edinburgh 2010)

25   Shawn Achor *The Happiness Advantage* (Virgin Books UK 2011)

26   Centre for Creative Leadership. "The 70-20-10 Rule for Leadership Development" www.ccl.org/articles/leading-effectively-articles/70-20-10-rule/

27   Daniel Pink *Drive* (Canongate Books, Edinburgh 2010)

28   Edwin A Locke (1996) "Motivation Through Conscious Goal Setting". *Applied and Preventative Psychology*. 5 (2): 117–24. www.sciencedirect.com/science/article/pii/S0962184996800059

29   Ken Blanchard and Spencer Johnson *The New One Minute Manager* (Thorsons, London 2015)

30   KPMG *Meet the Millennials* June 2017 https://home.kpmg.com/content/dam/kpmg/uk/pdf/2017/04/Meet-the-Millennials-Secured.pdf

31   Daniel Pink *Drive* (Canongate Books, Edinburgh 2010)

32   Stephen Mayson *Making Sense of Law Firms* (Blackstone Press Limited, London 1997) Chapter 32 Nature of Ownership

33   Luke Johnson in *The Sunday Times* 9 August 2015

34   MBTI – Myers Briggs Type Indicator. The Myers Briggs types suggest we have preferences in four areas: Introversion and Extraversion – how we each prefer to re-energise and focus – on the outer world or our inner world; Sensing and Intuition – how we prefer to take in information; Thinking and Feeling – how we prefer to make decisions; and Judging or Perceiving – do we like to make decisions early, or keep them open as long as possible? The four-type preferences sort into 16 personality types. These types are very widely used and can form a solid basis for getting to understand what makes people tick.

35 Our version of 'thinking rounds' is adapted from Nancy Kline *Time to Think* (Ward Lock, London 1999) Part Two 1 The Thinking Organisation Chapters 14, 15 and 16 pp 100–23

36 Quakers and Business Group "Quaker Methods for Decision Making" https://qandb.org/resources/publications/ethics-at-work/quaker-methods-for-decision-making

37 https://en.wikipedia.org/wiki/Albert_Mehrabian

38 Legal Cheek *The Firms Most List* – Most Target Hours www.legalcheek.com/the-firms-most-list/

39 PROCEED is my own – but it is based on a model given to me by Oonagh Harpur www.oonaghharpur.com/ and the MBTI Z model www.imperial.ac.uk/media/imperial-college/administration-and-support-services/staff-development/public/impex/Decision-making-using-MBTI.pdf

40 Bernice McCarthy *About Learning* (Excel Inc, Barrington Illinois, 1996)

41 Manfred Zimmermann "Fundamentals of Sensory Psychology" Chapter 3, Editor Robert F Schmidt *Neurophysiology of Sensory Systems* (Springer-Verlag 1986)

42 Tad James and Wyatt Woodsmall *Time Line Therapy and the Basis of Personality* (Meta Publications, Capitola USA, 1988) Introduction NLP Communication Model

43 Diane Ackerman "I Sing the Body's Pattern Recognition Machine". *The New York Times*, 15 June 2004 www.nytimes.com/2004/06/15/science/essay-i-sing-the-body-s-pattern-recognition-machine.html

44 Carolyn Gregoire "This is Scientific Proof That Happiness is a Choice." *The Huffington Post*, 9 December 2013 www.huffingtonpost.co.uk/entry/scientific-proof-that-you_n_4384433

45 Shawn Achor *The Happiness Advantage* (Virgin Books, UK 2011)

46 Clifton B Parker "Stanford Research: The Meaningful Life is a Road Worth Travelling". *Stanford Report*, 1 January 2014 https://news.stanford.edu/news/2014/january/meaningful-happy-life-010114.html

47 Matthew Walker *Why We Sleep* (Scribner, New York 2017)

48 National Sleep Foundation, Sleep Duration Recommendations https://sleepfoundation.org/sites/default/files/STREPchanges_1.png

49 www.headspace.com

50 Warren Buffet. Tipoff.com, Tipoff Inc, 2018. https://tipoff.com/quotes/warren-buffet/1000084

51 Dax Moy www.daxmoy.com/

52 Stephen Mayson *Making Sense of Law Firms* (Blackstone Press Limited, London 1997)

53 Stephen Mayson *Law Firm Strategy* (Oxford University Press, Oxford 2007)

54 Simon Sinek *Start with Why* (Portfolio Penguin, London 2011)

55 Simon Sinek *Leaders Eat Last* (Portfolio Penguin, London 2014)

56 Jim Collins and Jerry I Porras, *Built to Last*, 10th Anniversary Edition (Random House Business Books, London 2005)

57 Jim Collins *Good to Great* (Random House, London 2001

58 Patrick Lencioni *The Ideal Team Player* (Jossey-Bass, New Jersey 2016)

59 Patrick Lencioni *The Five Dysfunctions of a Team* (Jossey-Bass, San Francisco 2002)

60 David Maister *Managing the Professional Service Firm* (Simon & Schuster UK Ltd, London 2003)

61 Jay W Lorsch and Thomas J Tierney *Aligning the Stars: How to Succeed When Professionals Drive Results* (Harvard Business School Press, Boston 2002)

62 Daniel Pink *Drive* (Canongate Books, Edinburgh 2010)

63 Ruby Wax *Sane New World* (Hodder & Stoughton, London 2013)

64 Shawn Achor *The Happiness Advantage* (Virgin Books, UK 2011)

65 Shawn Achor *Before Happiness* (Virgin Books, London 2013)

12785986R00149

Printed in Great Britain
by Amazon